# POST ROAD

SUBMISSION AND SUBSCRIPTION INFORMATION

Post Road publishes twice yearly and accepts submissions in all genres.

• POETRY: Electronic submissions only at poetry@postroadmag.com.
*The title of the work(s) should appear in the email subject line and on the work(s) itself.*
*Please be sure that no identifying information appears on the manuscript. Microsoft Word*
*documents as attachments only. All other formats or submission of work in the body of an*
*email cannot be considered.*

• NONFICTION: Editor, Post Road, 203 Bedford Ave., Brooklyn, NY 11211

• FICTION: Electronic submissions only at fiction@postroadmag.com.
*The title of the work should appear in the email subject line and on the work itself. Please*
*be sure that no identifying information appears on the manuscript. Microsoft Word*
*documents as attachments only. All other formats or submission of work in the body of*
*an email cannot be considered.*

• ALL OTHER SUBMISSIONS should be addressed to the section editor and sent to:

Post Road
P.O. Box 400951
Cambridge, MA 02140

Subscriptions: Individuals, $16/year; Institutions, $32/year;
outside the U.S. please add $6/year for postage.

Post Road is a nonprofit 501(c)(3) corporation. All donations are tax-deductible.

Distributed by:
Bernhard DeBoer, Inc., Nutley, N.J.
Ingram Periodicals Inc., LaVergne, TN

PRINTED IN CANADA

www.postroadmag.com

# POST ROAD

*Founding Editors*
Jaime Clarke
David Ryan

*Managing Editor*
Mary Cotton

*Art Editor*
Susan Breen

*Criticism Editor*
Hillary Chute

*Etcetera Editors*
Josephine Bergin
Jaime Clarke
Alden Jones

*Fiction Editors*
Rebecca Boyd
Michael Rosovsky
David Ryan

*Nonfiction Editors*
Pete Hausler
Marcus McGraw

*Poetry Editors*
Mark Conway
Anne McCarty

*Associate Poetry Editor:* Jeffrey Shotts

*Recommendations Editor*
Tim Huggins

*Theatre Editor*
David Ryan

*Web Editor*
Ricco Villanueva Siasoco

*Web Designer*
Sean Dessureau

*Copy Editor*
Michelle Richards Peters

*Layout and Design*
Josephine Bergin

*Special thanks to:*
Catherine Parnell
Cheryl Reed

# Table of Contents

# Recommendations

# Etcetera

# Contributor Notes

**Ian Bickford's** poetry has appeared or is forthcoming in *LIT, CutBank, Smartish Pace*, the *Asheville Poetry Review, Spork*, and elsewhere. He lives in Brooklyn.

**Sven Birkerts** is the author, most recently, of *My Sky Blue Trades: Growing Up Counter in a Contrary Time*. He edits the journal *Agni* and is at work at a series of extended "encounters" with influential books.

**Ryan Boudinot's** work has appeared in *The Best American Nonrequired Reading 2003, The Mississippi Review*, and *Hobart*. He has written a novel about selling ice cream. He lives in Seattle.

**Joel Brouwer** is the author of two books of poems, *Exactly What Happened* and *Centuries*. He teaches at the University of Alabama.

**Christopher Castellani** studied literature in the graduate program at Tufts University. His first novel, *A Kiss from Maddalena*, was published in 2003 by Algonquin Books.

**Jim Dameron** considers himself an old-fashioned essayist. What the rest of the world thinks is an open question, but he has had essays published in *Northwest Review, Ascent*, and *River City*. He lives in Portland, Oregon.

**Dennis DiClaudio** lives in Philadelphia. He performs improvisational theater and edits for both *Ducky Magazine* and *(parenthetical note)*. His plays have been produced in New York City and Philadelphia, and his fiction has been published elsewhere.

**Angie Drakopoulos** is represented by g-module in Paris, and has exhibited at the NADA art fair-Miami beach, Art Rotterdam, GAle GAtes et al, dfn Gallery, Organization of Independent Artists and Woodward Gallery among others. She lives and works in New York City. Her artwork can be viewed at www.angiedrakopoulos.com.

**Sherry Ellis** coaches and teaches creative writing. Her interviews with Jill McCorkle and Lise Haines can be read in the online edition of *Agni*. Her interview with Paul Lisicky is published in *Provincetown Arts* 2003. She is at work on a novel.

**Maria Flook's** new novel, *Lux*, is forthcoming from Little, Brown and Co. in September 2004. Her other books include *Invisible Eden, A Story of Love and Murder on Cape Cod*, and *My Sister Life, The Story of My Sister's Disappearance*; the novels *Open Water* and *Family Night*; and the story collection *You Have the Wrong Man*. She is Writer-in-Residence at Emerson College.

**Derek Lance Furr** is a father, husband, writer and teacher living in Charlottesville, Virginia. He teaches for the Charlottesville City Schools and at the University of Virginia. His essays and poetry have been published in several periodicals, including *The New Delta Review, The Washington Post, The Potomac Review, English Language Notes*, and *The Cumberland Poetry Review*.

**Amy Gerstler's** most recent book of poems, *Medicine*, was published by Penguin Putnam in 2000. Her book *Ghost Girl* will be published by Penguin in April 2004. Her previous books include *Crown of Weeds* (Viking Penguin, 1997), *Nerve Storm* (Viking Penguin, 1993) and *Bitter Angel*, (North Point Press, 1990; Carnagie Mellon University Press, 1997).

**Gwendolen Gross** is the author of the novels *Field Guide* and *Getting Out*. *Book Magazine* has dubbed her "the reigning queen of women's adventure fiction," and despite that, she lives in New Jersey with her husband and two children.

**Daniel Hill** has shown his work at Lafayette College, Henry Street Settlement, GAle GAtes et al, and The National Arts Club. He received a BFA from Kent State University and an MFA from the School of Visual Arts. He lives and works in New York City. His artwork can viewed at www.danielhill.net.

**Virginia Holman** is the author of *Rescuing Patty Hearst*, a memoir of her mother's untreated schizophrenia. She has written for *DoubleTake, Self, Redbook, USA Today, The Washington Post, Glamour, Pushcart Prize* and others. She has recently received an Outstanding Literature Award from the National Alliance for the Mentally Ill, a Rosalynn Carter Fellowship in Mental Health Journalism, and a fellowship from the North Carolina Arts Council. She is currently the Kenan Visiting Writer at UNC-Chapel Hill.

**Nathan Ihara** has written about art, music, science, and chess for the *LA Weekly*. His short fiction appears online at eyeshot.net, sweetfancymoses.com, and opiummagazine.com. He will shortly earn his M.A. in creative writing at the University of Southern Mississippi's Center for Writers.

**Amy Kreines** was born in Long Island, New York and now lives in Boston, where she is pursuing a degree in writing at Emerson College.

**H. H. LeCraw** was born and raised in Atlanta. She has published work in *Edge City Review* and *The Boston Book Review*. She lives outside Boston with her husband and three children.

**Brian Lennon** is the author of *City: An Essay* (University of Georgia Press, 2001)."Some Stories Are Parables, But" is excerpted from *Post-Assassination*, a book-length prose sequence in progress.

**Risa Miller** is the author of *Welcome to Heavenly Heights* (St. Martin's Press, 2003), winner of a PEN Discovery Award, and lives in Brookline, Massachusetts.

**Ander Monson** lives in Michigan, where he edits the *New Michigan Press* and the online magazine *Diagram* (www.thediagram.com). His poetry manuscript, *Elegies for Descent and Dreams of Weather*, is forthcoming from Tupelo Press. Sarabande Books will publish his novel-in-stories, *Other Electricities*, in spring 2005.

**Rick Moody** is the author most recently of *Demonology* and *The Black Veil*.

**Mary Morris** is the author of 12 books, including five novels, three collections of short stories, three travel memoirs and, along with her husband, Larry O'Connor, an anthology of travel literature. The recipient of the Rome Prize in Literature, Morris teaches writing at Sarah Lawrence College. Her next novel, *Revenge*, will be published by St. Martin's next year.

**Tom Murphy**, a Carmelite, teaches English at Carmel High School in Mundelein, Illinois. His article on using indexes in the classroom has been published in *The Indexer*, the international journal of indexers. He may be found online at www.brtom.org.

**Taro Nettleton** is a Ph.D. student in the Visual and Cultural Studies program at the University of Rochester. In 2002, he curated *Just Like Music: Sound in the MCA Artists' Book Collection*, an exhibition held at the Museum of Contemporary Art in Chicago. He has been skateboarding since 1985.

**Thisbe Nissen's** new novel, *Osprey Island*, will be released by Knopf in 2004. She is the author of the collection *Out of the Girls Room and Into the Night* (Anchor Books) and the novel *The Good People of New York* (Knopf).

**Jude Nutter** is from North Yorkshire, England. She moved to the United States in the 1980's and spent 10 years homesteading on Wrangell Island in Alaska. She is a graduate of the M.F.A. Poetry Program at the University of Oregon, Eugene. Her poems have appeared in numerous international journals and anthologies and have been nominated three times for a Pushcart Prize. She is the recipient of several awards and grants, including a Minnesota State Arts Grant and The Marjorie J. Wilson Award for Excellence in Poetry. Her first book-length collection, *Pictures of the Afterlife*, was published by Salmon Poetry in 2002. In 2004 she will spend time in Antarctica as a participant in the National Science Foundation's Writers and Artists Program.

**Tom Perrotta's** new novel, *Little Children*, was recently published by St. Martin's Press. Perrotta is the author of four previous works of fiction—*Joe College*, *Election* (which was made into an acclaimed movie starring Matthew Broderick and Reese Witherspoon), *The Wishbones*, and *Bad Haircut*. He has taught writing at Yale and Harvard, and has worked as a screenwriter and journalist. His nonfiction work has appeared recently in *Rolling Stone* and *GQ*. He grew up in New Jersey and now lives outside Boston.

**Stephanie Pippin** holds a M.F.A. from Washington University in St. Louis where she is currently a Writer-in-Residence. Her poems have appeared in *Hayden's Ferry Review*, *Lyric Poetry Review*, and *Ploughshares*.

**Neal Pollack**, The Greatest Living American Writer, is the author of three books: the cult classic *The Neal Pollack Anthology of American Literature*, *Beneath The Axis Of Evil*, and the rock-n-roll novel *Never Mind The Pollacks*. His band, The Neal Pollack Invasion, no longer exists, but it had a glorious autumn. A columnist for *Vanity Fair* and a contributor to many other magazines, Pollack lives in Austin, Texas.

**Emma Ramey** is an Assistant Poetry Editor for *Diagram* and lives in the Seattle area.

**Lewis Robinson** is the author of *Officer Friendly and Other Stories* (HarperCollins). He has written essays for Maine Public Radio, *Sports Illustrated*, and *The Boston Globe* and his fiction has appeared in *Tin House*, *Open City*, *Shout*, and *The Missouri Review*. He lives in Portland, Maine.

**Lacy Schutz's** work has appeared or is forthcoming in *Fence*, *The Denver Quarterly*, *Seneca Review*, *Black Warrior Review*, *Gulf Coast*, *Mid-American Review*, and many other journals. She lives in Brooklyn.

**Liesl Schwabe** is currently an M.F.A. student in nonfiction at Bennington College. She lives in Brooklyn.

**Rachel Solar-Tuttle** is a writer, editor, writing advisor, and creative strategist. She is the author of the novel *Number Six Fumbles* (Pocket/MTV Books, 2002) as well as a new book, *Table Talk: The Savvy Girl's Alternative to Networking* (www.tabletalkbooks.com). Her work has appeared in *The Pennsylvania Gazette, The Harvard AIDS Review, Appeal, The Boston Globe,* and other publications. She lives with her husband Matt in Brookline, Massachusetts.

**Vincent Standley** is a writer and editor living in Providence, Rhode Island. Most recently his fiction has appeared in *The Denver Quarterly, Parakeet,* and *Quarterly West.*

**Mark Wunderlich** is the author of *The Anchorage,* and his second poetry collection, *Voluntary Servitude,* will be published in fall 2004 by Graywolf Press. He lives in Provincetown, Massachusetts.

# POETRY

POST ROAD

# Art and Literature, Together.

*Born Magazine* is an experimental venue for art and literature collaboration on the Web. Original projects are brought to life every three months, created by a continually evolving community of poets, writers, new media artists, programmers, photographers, and musicians. The magazine's work has been profiled in numerous magazines and online venues, including *The New York Times*, BBC online, and *Communication Arts*, and has received awards from The One Show, SXSW, *HOW Magazine*, and numerous Flash film festivals. *Born Magazine* is a nonprofit, volunteer organization founded in 1997.

WWW.BORNMAGAZINE.ORG

**bornmagazine**

# Device for Burning Bees and Sugar

Mark Wunderlich

It marks a grave.

Touch the sugar to your lips, ensuring its consistency, the amber pearl.

In the pan of hammered copper.

Collect the bees keeping in mind that on chill days or in fog, the hive remains sluggish. Wild bees offer distinct features, favoring thistle and columbine. Domestic bees are more still with essence of apple and clover bloom.

Release them from their trap into a bell jar. Fifty or sixty bees should suffice.

(Last night, the spring dream—finches beating the bars at the window, light mist.)

In the clearing, build a fire of dogwood and dung. A slow flame is required.

Prepare your text. Before you, many have come. Accordingly, the site you choose may well be a grave. Bodies pushed into the soil; bodies pushing up through the soil. Your text will be the needle point of remembrance. Belt this to your waist with the kidskin harness.

On the appointed morning bathe in water floated with white carnations.

Do this to satisfy the ghost.

Off and off and off.

As you read your text, the shadows will swell.

Release the bees one by one, feeding them into the device. As they touch the surface of the pan, the smoke will become a garment around you. In your hive of smoke, a calm will settle.

Inside you, a field will open outward.

The dead and their whispers cannot find you there

in a world of burning light and pollen.

# It's Your Turn to Do the Milking, Father Said

Mark Wunderlich

I spent a summer dancing on a bar. It was a summer of little daylight and I was mostly imaginary. Nights I sold my calves to strangers. They looked up at my white shorts and I blinked back, distant as a wren. Sometimes I smiled for their money. Sometimes I cared. In the back room, I counted the warm bills they tucked in my waistband, damp with small effort. I was infinitely expensive. My heart and head followed white lines to South America where jungle birds bloomed into shrieking hats. They beat inside my chest's bone cage, called so much into possibility—bar and boot and stray foreign hand.

As a boy, I was sent to bring in the goats. They were scattered in the hills, bleating, wet eyes narrowed, bells hollowing, udders dripping sweet blue. I called and they would not come. They had seen the serpent coiled in the loafing shed, his poison mouth sprung with needles. While it struck at my shins, I chopped it into pieces with a hoe, ground its vile head in the dust with my boot. I hung the mess in a sack from a post where it twisted until sundown. I made a hat band with its skin.

I am not as I would appear, you see. There is so much you never thought me capable of. The poor goats. I brought them in and milked them, they were so uncomfortable.

# Good Science

Stephanie Pippin

Judging by his letters I'd say this
Is a man who knows
Something of wings & extinction.


On the edge of spring,
Even before the flowers
Can rise & pucker like scars,
He names me Lonely.
What spine, what good
Science takes him far from my alchemy
Of locket & rosewater?
Here we go on thanking
God the island's small.

I wear this weave of him,
Hair at my wrist closing me
Off like January's clench


When the water rolls,
A god's eye, under ice.
What portents I decipher


From these creases.
They smell of fair weather.
They smell of jungle.


I dream of his fingers probing
Deep in the moist soil.
His hands hold orchids, hold

A nest of speckled eggs.
I write back to say—
*I will unlove you, tenderly,*

*The way your birds learn*
*To unlove this ground*
*& leave it amazed.*

# Heart

Stephanie Pippin

I wanted something whorish
and hard-driven, a Queen
in a short reign,
a zoo wolf unmuzzled,
on parole from her cage.


I imagined the color—
a puddle of flush, of stop
and seduce, red as a filched lipstick.
It is not what I expected, this heart—
Shotgun target, it throbs
like a girl at a dance.


It opens and shuts like a doll's eye.
My hands are a different story.
They can hold on
to bits of you, or wander
pharmacies, filling themselves
with candies and aspirin.


They can say *closed* and mean *fist*.

# The Wings of Butterflies

Jude Nutter

The British artist Damien Hirst has found controversy again. This time it
is not for his pickled sheep or sharks floating in tanks of formaldehyde,
but for a new piece, "Amazing Revelations," a triangular collage made of
thousands of dismembered butterfly wings.

*New York Times*, August 19th, 2003

These are not the insects of our childhoods—
the common beauties we painted, open-winged
on their favourite flowers, their native landscapes
in the background marching away: Mourning Cloak,
Brimstone, Adonis Blue. What hangs before
me is the map to a world of many thousand territories
I cannot name. But there are voices everywhere: wings
like mouths held open around a single hue—thalo,
manganese, Prussian, cerulean—blues that slip out of us
when we are sleeping; and here and there a green
so fanciful it's like a door left open under the grass.
Such beauty is the aftermath of terrible violence,
and because there are wings here with hems of copper
that keep burning, but slightly, like the troubled air
around a moving bullet, my mind wanders
to John James Audubon in long silk stockings and fancy
satin breeches shooting his way through Pennsylvania
in the name of art, passing wires
through the bodies of birds and then posing
each one carefully; and only then taking up his brushes
and his palette to prove—no matter how hard,
or how long it took—that death,

not art, imitates life. It is said that butterflies
release faint odours, and that males have more pleasing
perfumes than females—among them, red clover
and fresh honey. How many ways can there be to separate
a pair of wings from a body? In my mind
there are bevies of schoolboys racing every Friday

after class to the artist's greenhouse where the weekly,
afternoon shipment has been released. Beneath their clothes,
the boys are hairless, unmuscled; they leave their satchels
and books outside on the grass. What do they make
of these new animals they keep creating that ripple
up the glass and among the terracotta pots of parsley
and mint like small, dark thumbs?
The lawns beyond the greenhouse are manicured

and formal; no emotion anywhere and O, I think,
let a handful of girls step through the green nimbus
of the lilac, break from the clasp of leaf light into the open;
let them be dressed in gingham skirts and white blouses,
in shifts of blue cotton; let those boys feel love's
soft knock on the breastbone and hesitate for only
a moment before turning away
from their terrible work. Let them turn away

from their terrible work. But it will not happen.
Here I am, in a gallery in a city of the civilized world
and even the view through the window's like a painting,
albeit a Sunday afternoon by Seurat with sunbathers
scattered like sweets on the grass, and a dog, trailing
its leash, running free through the park, and the river
releasing and replacing its own long body;
and before me, this wall of shimmering evidence—
wings like face cards, flakes of mica, chips of spruce
bark and Roman tile; like snips of silk, like dresses
too beautiful to wear. Stolen coats of coloured dust. Proof
that even the worst things we can imagine
do happen. I know I should be thinking about the slag
heaps of shoes at Chelmno and Auschwitz, at Sobibor
and Treblinka; about skulls gathered up like stones,
from the soils of Rwanda, the soils of Bosnia,
from the soils of El Salvador and Cambodia; about the victims
of wars in eight out of every ten countries I can name,
and how a hundred, a thousand, a hundred-thousand,

a million can be herded to a common fate and yet
each death will be different. But all I can think of
is how only yesterday, in the aftermath of a bomb blast
at a market in Mumbai, among the strewn, charred wreckage
and shredded bodies, rescuers found other debris—whole
pineapples, oranges, sweet limes.

# The Eyes of Fish

Jude Nutter

I walk beneath the trees through a house
of green fire, down across the rocks and the locked,
blue closets of the mussels to where the sockeye
are bottlenecked at the mouth of the river
under the great footfall of the sun,
in water canorous with their desire.
They have travelled, without choice, for years,
back to the salmagundi of leaf-light and shadow
in the river's rills and braids, where the waters
still smell like the leaves of geraniums, like furred
and quiet coughings in the soil, like precious metals.
I could walk across the bay on the raft they make
with the fire and spackle of their bodies, and it's easy

to see how two of them, in the hands of a prophet,
once satisfied us in such numbers.
There are many kinds of hunger,
and slipping into water is like coming home,
to great welcome, after an argument,
so in my mask and fins and my brand-new skin
I swim through their ranks of flame. I tell you
there is something immense—like the dark
inside mirrors and cathedrals, like a forest
seen at night from a train—inside the eyes of fish;
that behind the armoured portal of every
single gill plate winks the luminous, wistful signal
of the gills like something partly forbidden—the pale
flash of underwear of girls turning cartwheels
on their lawns in summer, or glints, perhaps,
and glimpses of the dead in their ceaseless vigils
behind every one of a thousand doors
suddenly standing ajar. When there's nothing

in the world to write about, said Rilke, we must write
about our dreams and fears. But what happens if the world
itself is our dream. And our fear. And our fear
is that we vanish like they do—dreaming of home,
mouthing for air, driven, starving, dressed
in crimson. One among many. Like a luff
of radiance when the wind turns
towards shore at evening. And our dream, of course,

is the same.

# And the Ship Sails On

Joel Brouwer

He faced the sink, one foot up
on the edge of the tub. She stood
behind him, reaching around.
In the mirror, her face rose
over his shoulder like the moon,
and like the moon she regarded him
beautifully but without feeling,
and he looked at her as he would
at the moon: *How beautiful!*
*How distant!* No smiling, no giggling,
no talking. A man and a woman
transacting their beautiful business
with the usual equanimity. The man
as a passenger walking the ship's deck
at evening and the woman as the moon
over his shoulder oiling the ocean
with light. Deep in the ship's belly
pistons churned and sailors fed
the boilers' roar with coal. On deck
just the engine's dull thrum and
a faint click as the woman sets her ring
on the cold white lip of the sink.

# Beckett's *Endgame*

Joel Brouwer

The steps, the biscuit, the glass, the powder,
the dog, the gaff, the clock. If we lost
our way we skipped to "take me for a turn,"
but we preferred everything in order, in
its last place under its last dust, and so
penciled our margins with vigor. Earth, weeping,
ocean, wedding. The June of ukases, when
Henrik averred that the fireflies had so
over-bred they were no longer lovely.
Yes, "Henrik averred." There's English for you.
Rehearsals slipped from light Spanish red to
jumbo bourbons to cosmetologists
from the storefront next door pounding the walls
with scissors and conditioners.
And then slipped deeper into the evenings,
like seeds seeking water. We scratched around
our seeds to see if they'd sprouted. They would
never sprout. Mindy wired the lights, Zack
made plans for Madagascar with Francine
on his lap, and I memorized my lines—
my *mene mene* lines—down by the lake,
jaundiced among lustrous, unlovely swarms.
Which is a fancy way to say our seeds
would never sprout. Which is a folksy way
to say we were trying to sell ourselves
into slavery as quickly as we could,
but no one was buying. Which is true.
When we stepped out of character to comfort
the weepers—*It's a comedy!*—they leapt
from their chairs to terrify us: *It isn't!*
What skilled attention we got, we dying
of our wounds, we the glowing smear in summer's palm.

# Servant

Emma Ramey

What was I but an eyelash. Just the boy's breath and I was gone, into the air of thirst and garlic. Who was it that saw me, anyway. Chin to my chest. Not even the boy, so close, nor the voices, addressing me. What was I but a direction. Of sound, of orders. The superiority of wealth. But then, my response: the glimpse of that boy's back, in the river.

# Servant

Emma Ramey

I dreamt of this: the prosthesis on the boy. The knee that didn't bend and the boy as the circle's compass. But the boy would never walk a perfect circle, just a chain, the repeated curve of defect. This dream and that boy. The boy, who had never said a word, never even looked my way. And yet the boy's skin was a watercolor, and his youthful splashes in the river inspired laughter, and there was not one set of eyes that did not at some point linger, smile at the sight of him. Then there was me and, yes, I made a cripple in my dream and, no, I am not proud that it was this that let me sleep.

# Excision

**Ander Monson**

Photographs of you through the ice
the black and whites in the Gazette
of your machine being craned
up from the canal.

Here's one of ice like a scar
that has to be cracked back open
like a car crash windshield
fixed in the night.

Kids on the bridge.
The body's return
on a gurney. Its skin not blue
but dark like a bruise.
A shot of the shroud.

The paper's smell
of oil and ink.

One of the boil on the ice,
the gap, the wet gate
from a cancerous life
of bars, dull adrenaline
haze, and drunken
punches taken in the chest
like shots, a convenient job
at the Citgo station
selling liquor to teens.

A route out, one of few.

When is incision necessary to unzip the skin,
clear the way for removal? When
does a mole fatten, go oblique
like a ship or shocked whale,
turn lesion, tumor, malignant?
When must it be cut, burned, or frozen
whatever the cost to the body?

# Limb Replantation, Failed

Ander Monson

They're not like crops, your forearms.
Your elbows never laid fallow
awaiting the season when again
they would be tilled, and bear up grain.

This is what is done
when the limb is completely cut—no nerves intact,
no tightrope, no high wire act
to string the tissue to the body.

We learned in Physical Science
that Work is Force times Distance
that the body is a mechanism
the arm an urn of gears and pivot

and all the while
the bastards in the back
consumed their glue with hands
contained their glee like pee in jars

their hairs rode high like pikes
stuck in a jack-o-lantern
rotted half away on the porch
after Halloween.

What are the laws that govern pain
corollaries fitted to the bone of distribution?
Where is the equal and opposite
reaction to your loss?

What good, mitosis?
What is it but a spreading out
of end? Why the mucous membrane
of the cell, so like a killing jar?

To what purpose, apogee
and crown of sun, you awful Sputnik
crashing answerless
back into earth, into the sea?

# ART

## POST ROAD

# Daniel Hill: Paintings

Introduction by Lacy Schutz

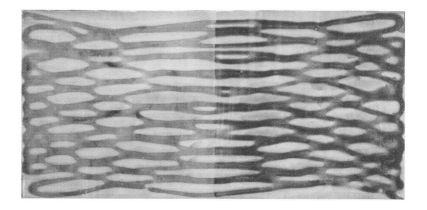

I often find myself wanting to experience things through my tongue. Things benign (the edge of my coffee cup before I take the first sip) and inappropriate (the metal bar in the subway car, the Giacometti sculptures at the Met). It springs from a desire to experience things without an intermediary. When I first saw Daniel Hill's artwork, I wanted to put my tongue on it, have some other experience of the art. Draw it into myself through means other than my eyes.

If something tasted blue to me, or something sounded like apricots, I would be experiencing synesthesia. From the Greek. Syn = together. Aisthesis = To perceive. To perceive together. A union of the senses. My desire to taste art is a kind of synesthesia, a desire to apprehend it via a sense other than sight. Taste. Hearing. Touch. We rarely get to touch art. I'm no more able to put my fingertips on the Giacometti sculptures than I am able to press my tongue to their rough surfaces. And if I were able to, what would I find but the cold taste of metal, dust?

And what would we hear if we could experience one of Hill's paintings or drawings through the ears? Hill is also a musician and composer. One of the first things you notice in these pieces is the allusion to sound waves. Some of the pieces have a sort of doubleness to them, a kind of stereo effect that mimics the way we see with two eyes, hear with two ears. Sound and sight both wrap around us—sound waves and peripheral vision both bend to each side of our bodies.

But beyond these visually apparent forms, there is a deeper reference to minimalist music. Composers like John Cage, Lamont Young,

Steve Reich, et al. have drawn from non-western approaches to composition. In Indian music, for instance, there are three prominent aspects to a piece of music: the tala, the raga and the drone. The tala is the rhythmic pattern, while the raga is the melodic pattern. The drone is a tonic, the sustained sound that links everything together.

The drone, especially by itself, creates a kind of trance. It is mantric and hypnotic. It slows down the mind which in turn opens up the ability to perceive cycles of time in a different way. Hill's work manifests this and other notions of minimalist music. Minimalist composers are led fully neither by control nor chance, but attempt some middle ground, an unedited performance both within and without musical structures. As Hill works, he strives for the same sort of candid, performative feeling. There is a compositional structure to the pieces—their lines, colors. But in the end, the work telegraphs the trance-like state of its maker and if the viewer has the leisure to meditate upon one of these pieces, it is possible to fall inside, fall into a pendulum-like swing as the lines seem to move both rhythmically and melodically from side to side.

There is a sort of beautiful problem to being an artist in any genre and it is the desire to transcend one form and carry it into another. Perhaps it is overly simple to apply the notion of synesthesia to this dilemma. As people who communicate in a lingua franca of creativity, whether it be song, poetry, sculpture or painting, we long to cross into another territory: the singer who wants to write poems; the writer's desire to sing on a stage; my own sometimes wish that I could replace my pens and blank pages with paint encrusted, mangled tubes of acrylics and oils. At the end of the day, however, the song is strengthened by the poem, the poem is enlarged by the painting, and the painting takes us to undreamed of new territories on the back of a single, sustained note.

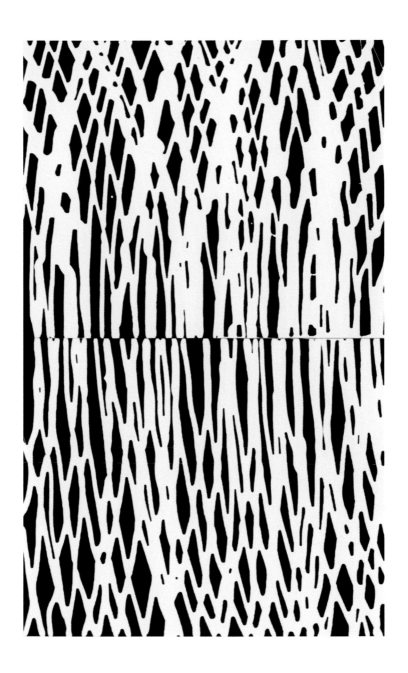

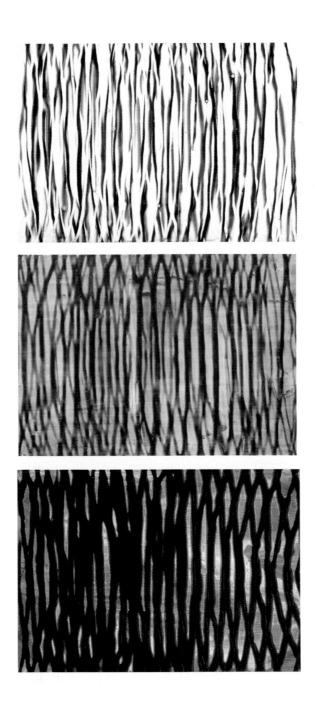

# Angie Drakopoulos: Paintings

Introduction by Ian Bickford

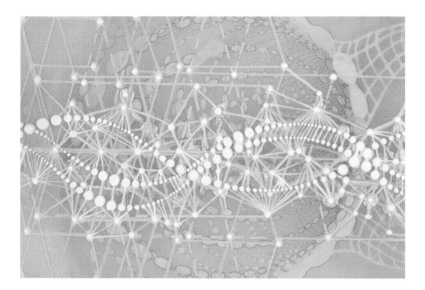

**W**hen you lean toward the surface of the resin, there follows a solid second during which you don't know where to stop. This is an old feeling, antique, embarrassed, yet buried in a new astonishment—its origins in that early moment when your first set of second lips were bombing toward you and you suddenly realized, to your alarm, that you'd never really thought about the blunt, relentless *fact* of your face. Awful: your brow a hull-like bulge, your nose-tip a treasonous agent that, you understood before it happened, would block the finish of this forbidden gesture. Meanwhile new distances multiplied in front of you. It was a landscape of cells and crystals. You bit your tongue and yelped. You wanted in.

There's a line from one or another of Richard Powers's novels: you'll shrink to nothing in the size of this, but you will not disappear.

Or there's the thing that physicist David Bohm was sure of, the belief that motivated his imagination of a quantum universe: physical existence is participatory, it is whole, and you can feel every law of it in your body.

Angie Drakopoulos makes art as though she were trying to reassemble a world whose pieces have been splintered against the bulwark of the history of human thought and scattered over time to the partisanship of context and discipline. Under Drakopoulos's guidance, physics meets and merges with metaphysics. Astronomy remembers its kinship to the zodiac. Mathematics absorbs and is absorbed by philosophy. Chemistry warms to alchemy. Logic welcomes myth. Nowhere does hard science surrender an inch of its precision, nor does the uncanny recant its magic. Rather, in these multilayered, multidimensional collages, discrete symbolic systems are reconciled as simultaneous and therefore related. They fade into each other, measuring themselves against the thousand shapes and possibilities spiraling in all directions. They disappear into each other's background. They become impossible to sort.

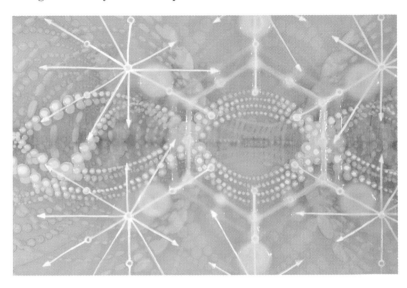

In other words, Drakopoulos's work is given wholly to the chance of seeing around corners. When light hits these pieces, from one angle and then from another, feverish hints emerge from far inside of shapes that— you're sure—will profoundly change the significance of the shapes floating more boldly near the surface. The result is a longing to see behind, to peer into the substratum, to position your body at a perfect diagonal that will lead you straight back to the foundation of all these layers—that will deliver you to the source. It's a wish that betrays its own limitations. You know you'll collide with some other journeying body. And here, here is Drakopoulos's real insight: any exploration, any theory, any rubric of faith or art or science is at its center an exercise in interrupted travel. Eventually organic molecular structures, say, will equal—will indeed become indistinguishable from—even the largest orbital diagrams of galaxies and nebulae because they each enter our range of perception via the narrow roads of human sense and material experience. We can crane our necks and squint. We can trade our telescopes for microscopes. There will always be bodies in the path of our bodies, shining and moving, sending our light back to us.

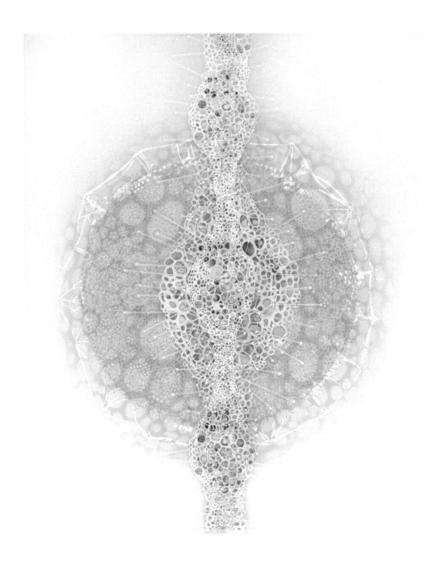

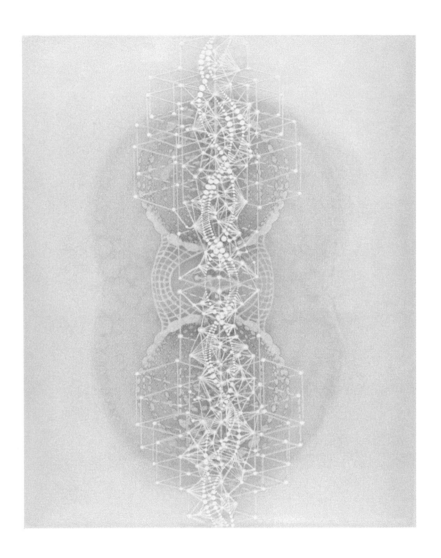

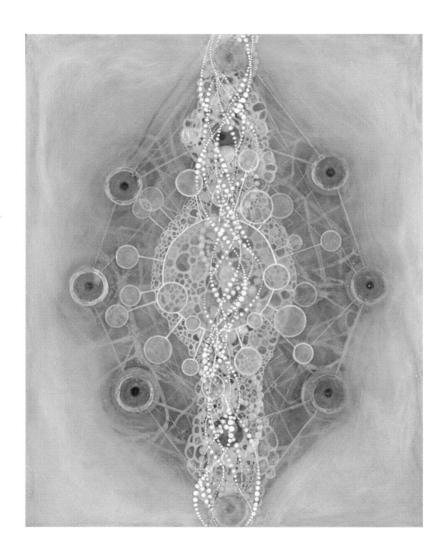

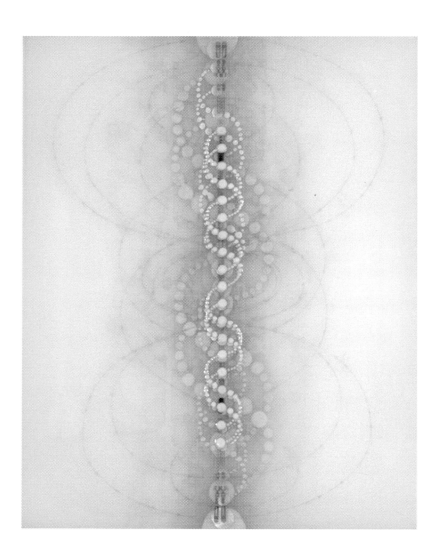

## Daniel Hill: Paintings

Page 34, Untitled (blue & red diptych #1), acrylic, 8" x 12", 2003

Page 35, Untitled (yellow & white), enamel, 17" x 14", 2003

Page 36, Untitled (yellow diptych), enamel, 17" x 28", 2003

Page 37, Untitled (yellow & black diptych), acrylic & enamel,
   14" x 24", 2003

Page 38, Oveon #1, acrylic, 100" x 53", 2003

Page 39, Set #1, #2, #3, acrylic, 10.5" x 8.25" (each), 2002

Page 40, Untitled (red & blue diptych #2), enamel, 17" x 28", 2003


## Angie Drakopoulos: Paintings

Page 41, Sequence III (Detail), Mixed media and resin on wood, 2003

Page 42, Sequence IV (Detail), Mixed media and resin on wood, 2003

Page 43, Sequence VII, Mixed media and resin on wood, 13" x 16",
   2003

Page 44, Sequence III, Mixed media and resin on wood, 13" x 16", 2003

Page 45, Sequence VI, Mixed media and resin on wood, 13" x 16", 2003

Page 46, Sequence IV, Mixed media and resin on wood, 13" x 16", 2003

Page 47, Sequence I, Mixed media and resin on wood, 13" x 16", 2003


Note: The orientation of all pieces shown is horizontal.

# FICTION

POST ROAD

# Some Stories Are Parables, But

Brian Lennon

■ ■ ■ when I got up from the porch, at the party on the farm, at which I could not speak, I looked out over the cornfield with stacked fluffy clouds and strings of sun and sprinklers and distant pickups trailing dust, at which I stared for a while, then I left, and when I got up from the porch I lost my composure, there was a dog there, and a small child, and a larger retarded child, and some people that I knew, whom I was glad to see. The dog ate potato chips, its head in the bag, the smaller child placed insects on the turntable, while the larger retarded child walked in circles on the porch making alarming sounds. I looked out over the field, I thought I'd seen an elephant but it was nothing, I lost my composure then. It was easy to regret, being glad to see people, for example if your motives are weak, if you're lonely, or if you're desperate for distraction from yourself, which deforms the other person, or if you give in out of guilt, because someone else is lonely or desperate for distraction, and you mislead or are misled by someone, in which case you are lonelier than before, because rather than wandering in darkness you are pinned under a vivisecting light, and then there's a struggle, which always turns out badly, in shame and raging at yourself: "Damn me!" Of course I'm exaggerating, but when we moved out here from the city, a thousand miles, we thought we'd be glad to see people. At the party, I was itching to leave, to return to the city, or maybe I was just watching the larger retarded child when I saw the elephant, I looked out at the corn, an elephant raising dust, it was nothing, or it was a truck, though what truck would be draped with gold braid, now I remember what I was thinking. I was thinking of the passage in Heidegger that reads, "Anxiety brings Da-sein face to face with its Being-free for the authenticity of its Being," which of course means everything and nothing, and in any case is not party conversation, but I wanted to be at a party at which one could say, "Anxiety brings Da-sein face to face with its Being-free for the authenticity of its Being," and I was deploring the scarcity of such parties, when I saw the elephant. Who is really ever happy at a party? When I was a child, another child vomited in the camp pool, a menacing slick spread over the water, oozing my way. I jumped out just in time, the perp cried while they hosed him down, I went behind a bush and I vomited too, when I came out the child who had vomited first was on his knees, blubbering, spitting and vomiting, and then one after another little classmate, observing, removed a finger from a nose and vomited too, the place was awash in it, our "counselors" were horrified, one child had been vomited on by several of the rest, he looked awful, it dripped from him into the pool, he fell in, started thrashing around, and the counselors looked at each other, but they jumped in, it was a mess, everyone vomited that day, even the "principal," who came to find out what was going on. To this day, when someone gets in front of me and opens his mouth, I worry there is vomit on the way. The elephant plodded along, determined or bored or weary or disconsolate, on a road I couldn't see, it was raising dust, so it had to be on a road, and I looked away and then looked back again and it was gone. But once when I was in Nevada I saw a train of elephants, holding each other's tails, dropping them, trumpeting, it may have been a heat mirage, who knows, I was crawling on my stomach moaning "Agua!" so I wasn't in very good shape, that was when I was a Bedouin, though Bedouins don't speak Spanish, I must've been mixed up, when I got home from the party it occurred to me I should go for a walk, to clear my head of Heidegger, so out and down the sidewalk, the houses on our street were dark, was everyone out or just asleep, hard to tell, was everyone at the party, suddenly I tripped on a branch, I stopped and picked up the branch and threw it on the top of the hedge, but first I looked around, to see if anyone were watching, because I didn't want anyone to see, then I picked up the branch and threw it on the top of the hedge, and walked on. The meaning of the passage in Heidegger I took to be, when you are anxious you are closest to the point of overcoming your anxiety, which means everything and nothing, and suddenly it occurred to me that the branch, which I threw on the hedge so that no one else might trip on it, might be projecting over the sidewalk, at neck level, and that it might stick someone in the neck. I hadn't considered the branch's position, I just wanted it off the walk, besides it was dark, I wanted to move on, to clear my head, but what if it projected over the walk, what if someone came along, were injured in the neck, neck injury is serious, so I had to reverse my steps, the branch was pointing into the walk, it nearly stuck me in the neck, so I dragged it down, threw it back where it was before. But I was doing all this without my leg, the leg I left behind, which remained on the porch when I got up, so I was hopping, I hopped down the darkened street, tripped over the branch, hopped on, hopped back and dragged it from the hedge, and standing on the porch, looking out over the field, the passage from Heidegger came to mind, and since it was the only thing in my mind, and since what was in my mind was unsayable, that's to say everything and nothing, and in any case not party conversation, perhaps its meaning at last ran clear, perhaps I understood— though this of course is only speculation.  ✧

# August

H. H. LeCraw

He was seventy-eight years old, and could not remember ever being in a toy store. It was early August, sultry, Harvard Square alive with the false busyness of tourists and summer school students. The semester wouldn't start for another six weeks. Tomorrow, he and Cookie were going to Italy, the morning flight; nevertheless, today Paul had found himself out walking, time on his hands. He stood at the window of the store, a place he'd passed dozens of times without stopping, now entranced by the bright objects in the window—a rideable firetruck, circling trains, a spinning ferris wheel made of interlocking plastic pieces, as high as his head. He was not sure if toys this fantastic had existed when he was a boy or not. Slowly, he walked to the door and pushed it open.

Inside it was cool, with a clean, wholesome smell, entirely different from the rubber-and-chemical odor of the hardware store a block away (still, thankfully, a useful place), or the linty scent of the haberdasher's around the corner, where he had been buying ties for the past forty years. There were two steps up into the store. He negotiated them well. The knee was holding up; that young Dr. Harris did solid work. His knee, however, a new creation of Gore-tex and plastic, was surely not as artful as that small garbage truck over there, with the cunning levers and the open driver's door. He walked closer to inspect it. There was a garbage man clinging to this door with a miniature hand, his own plastic knee bent, ready to hoist himself into his truck and continue on his way, an eternal smile of uncomplicated cheer on his tiny face.

A woman was approaching him, smiling also. Reflexively, he put his hands behind his back and glanced at the closest merchandise (boxed-up trucks piled high, a dollhouse on the top shelf), as though he knew what he was doing, was, perhaps, on a specific errand but only mildly interested in what he saw here. It was a skill of his to let people know, in an entirely courteous way, that he did not need or want their opinions. He wouldn't know, anyway, what to say to a woman who sold toys. Still smiling, she was moving away. She could have been one of his daughters-in-law; she was in her thirties, settled but still young. Pretty. Curly blonde hair, like his sister had had, long ago, Mamie, there was a name you never heard anymore, Mamie who had stayed in Florida and had died of cancer when she was twenty-three. The toy woman was the age person he found difficult to talk to now. An age Mamie had never got to. Thirties and forties—people who seemed to know so much more than he did, to be able to move so much faster. He remembered how he had felt when he was that woman's age, full of possibility, yet in control.

From a polite distance the toy woman was looking at him again, her smile now a question, and he realized he had been standing in the same spot for too long.

He roused himself and began to inspect the displays in earnest. The trucks—what an amazing array, and what detail! All manner of earth mover, fire trucks with ladders and without, the little garbage truck, ambulances, harvesters. All made of plastic, but they seemed to be quite sturdy, quite a high quality plastic. European, of course—the toys. Exacting, the Europeans were. He admired that, always had, the way they had of requiring the highest standards.

A wooden train set on a low table, with a roundhouse and bridges and tunnels, all of nicely finished wood. Birch, possibly, or ash. Did they make things of ash anymore? In the next bay over, dolls; nearby, high chairs, cribs, strollers, a good English pram. Better construction than Cookie's little Japanese car. Paul had a daughter; had Marian ever played with dolls like this? Hard to remember. Had she—or the boys—had they looked like these infant dolls, their foreheads wide and serious, their mouths pursed between round expanses of cheek, fingers fat and creased, newly hatched? They must have; pictures would tell him they had. Jean would remember. That had been her thing, he had left it to her.

It had been long enough now that it took only a nanosecond to remember he could not ask Jean, so little time that it was seamless to him, as if he were doing no remembering at all; just a slight tick in the flow of his thought; and any sadness he might have left was subsumed in that tick, so that he no longer had to register it, adjust to it yet again. He did not remember Jean often now as anything more than a fact; he had Cookie.

He had never bought gifts for his grandchildren. That had been Jean. They had money enough from him to keep them comfortable for years to come, so he had no cause to feel guilty. And they had toys, he had seen them, plastic rubbish that would shatter if you happened to step on it, proto-computer contraptions that even sounded badly made, with their tinny beeping and clicking. Cookie didn't care for toys either; or children, for that matter; she was charming with them but even he had to admit she did not feel their absence in her life. No, he had no need to buy anyone a thing.

But in the next little bay was a shelf of toys he finally could not resist touching. There was a car, a boat on wheels, and a train, bigger than the one on the table, pulling two cars. All the toys were wooden, bright as Life Savers, their sturdy corners rounded and their finish thick and glossy. The train was the best. It had a silver bell on top of the engine, and its cars held pegs carrying stacks of colored disks, which he removed, one by one. For a moment, he fought the urge to put one in his mouth. They had a satisfying click and heft, like currency from some sunny country where transactions were simple and straightforward. *One green disk, my darling,* he thought, as if it were a line from an old song, *green as leaves in May, and I will buy you happiness.*

He kept better track of his grandchildren's birthdays than one might expect; knew the months, anyway; little Jonathan would be having a birthday soon. He would be three, or perhaps four. He clicked the disks thoughtfully. He had been in the hospital for some time after he was born, Jonathan had, an early baby, and he, Paul, had gone to see him and had been stunned at his tininess and the little plexiglass house in which he slept and the tube running into his nose. Jean was gone by then; Cookie had accompanied him to the hospital. He had been proud to squire her on this family errand, proud that the nurses had granted the two of them admittance, but when he had beheld his grandson's utter helplessness he had not known what to say, and had been completely uninterested in any observations Cookie had to make. It had been, as a matter of fact, a moment of terror: he had felt, as he had not before or since, a sudden contempt for her and her ideas.

But now Jonathan was a big strapping boy, handsome, a little shy, not compliant about sitting on Paul's lap, if Paul happened to request it. Turning three or four, and he was sure it was August; he remembered driving to the hospital with Cookie, the waves of heat rising from the asphalt of the hospital parking lot, in the first heady days of their courtship.

He replaced the disks and picked up the whole train, the bell dinging faintly, and carried it to the register. The smiling blonde woman came to meet him. "You've found something," she said. "This company has such lovely things. Swiss. So well made." Paul felt unexpectedly pleased that he and the toy woman had some common ground, after all. "Someone is going to be very happy," she said, and began to hunt for the price tag.

"My grandson," Paul said. "He's turning three this month." He humphed, cleared his throat. "Or perhaps it's four." He smiled at the woman; she would forgive him this lapse.

But she was putting down her scanner. "I see." Professional concern clouded her face. "You know, this toy is really designed for a baby. Developmentally speaking. Eye-hand coordination, cause and effect, you know." She smiled sympathetically. "I'm afraid a three-year-old would outgrow it quite quickly. And a four-year-old would want nothing to do with it."

He tried to remember himself at four. He wanted to tell her that he would have felt nothing but delight at receiving such a thing. But now, apparently, children were different. They were highly advanced. They had exacting standards.

He let the woman sell him one of the trucks from the front of the store—not the garbage truck set out for display, somehow he did not have the temerity to request that one, but an earthmover, still in its box. It came with a tiny wheelbarrow and construction men and minuscule tools for them to hold. Fifteen minutes earlier, he would've been quite pleased with it. But when he found himself back on the sidewalk in the heat, he felt bereft.

He began to walk homeward. Perhaps it was simply odd to be without Cookie. He often went on errands without her, but they were quick, familiar, predetermined, the cobbler or dry-cleaner, or the bakery to buy the almond cookies he must have on hand. Today, she was playing tennis with Doris Coolidge; she expected him home later in the afternoon, to pack. Italy had been his idea. Cookie had laughed at the idea of going in August ("Sweetie, it will be crawling with Germans and Japanese—and the heat!"), but had agreed in the end. He had not been back, astonishingly, since the war.

Superbly organized, was Cookie; she could play tennis, have a lunch date the day before a three-week trip; then the afternoon would be an efficient flurry, Cookie drawing out foreign adapters and collapsible walking sticks and extra film from well-marked storage boxes, collecting his medicines, rolling his trousers in the ingenious way she had so that when they arrived in Rome, *ecce!* they would emerge unwrinkled, creases intact. That night they were to have dinner with the Baldwins, their suitcases clasped shut and ready by the door at home. Yes, Cookie kept him on a marvelous schedule. He knew full well that without her he would drift, would, quite literally, wither and die.

So he was not expected home until, say, two o'clock—although Cookie would suppose him to be home now, having his usual soup, then taking a nap. But it was already noon, and he had this bag, this truck, this piece of heavy equipment, weighing in his hands. He would have to deliver the toy to Jonathan today. His step quickened, and he turned off Brattle Street onto Hawthorn. If he had one of those cell phones, he could call Jennifer, his daughter-in-law, to make sure they were home; but he did not. He did not want, anyway, to be dissuaded. His hurry was greater than he had realized, and when he reached his own driveway he headed straight for his car.

It took only minutes to drive from Harvard Square to Belmont. He thoroughly approved of Teddy's decision to buy a house here, approved of the house itself, neither too big nor too small, a sensible investment, just as he approved of most things Teddy did. He was Paul's youngest son, the one who resembled Paul most closely in personality, although in looks he was all Jean. Yet it occurred to Paul, as he drove, that perhaps Teddy was not aware of the extent of Paul's approval. Or, perhaps, that he didn't care. He hadn't seen Teddy and Jennifer in weeks—couldn't remember the last time. Well, it was a good thing he was going today.

The house was on a leafy side street, a brick Colonial, flowers lining the front walk, raggedy now in August. There were toys scattered on the front lawn—more plastic. He had thought Jennifer ran a pretty tight ship. She had the two little boys now. Jonathan and the baby, Willie. William had been his own father's name. When Willie was born—full-size— Teddy had emphasized that there were Williams on Jennifer's side too. Paul didn't know why Ted would be so eager to dilute his act of homage. For himself, he persisted in ignoring the fact of these other ghostly Williams.

He was standing on the steps ringing the bell when he realized that he could have bought the little train for Willie. Regret knocked him in the chest so hard that he gasped. Just then, Jennifer answered the door. "Paul! What a surprise—are you okay? What's wrong?" She reached out as if to catch him. Maybe he had gone pale too.

"Oh, fine, fine," he squeezed out. "Hello, dear." He reached for her shoulder in a half-hug, leaned on her a little too hard, but by the time they had parted again he was steady. He held up the bag from the toy store. "Brought a little something for the birthday boy."

Jennifer's pretty face was blank for a moment. Then, "Of course! Jonathan. Are you sure you're all right? Come in, come in. His birthday is in a couple of weeks."

"Well, we'll be in Italy, you see." How nicely that worked out. He was beginning to feel much better. He crossed the threshold into the entrance hall. More toys, and a stack of folded laundry on the steps. He looked around expectantly.

"Oh, he's not here," Jennifer said. "He's at a playdate. One of his best little friends. If we'd known you were coming—" A shade of disapproval crossed her face.

"I see." Yes, these little children, even they had schedules now. He was familiar with this from his older grandchildren, how if you happened to stop by they would not be gathered in the kitchen doing homework around the table or playing in the yard, but instead off at soccer or violin or clay class. Even little Jonathan, at three, or four. No sense to be disappointed. "Well, there's the other one," Paul said. "The little one." He peered over her shoulder. "Young William."

Jennifer's face softened. "Yes, indeed. Come on in here." She led him into the kitchen, which was attached to a sunny playroom. Good God, more toys. A low red-and-green kitchen set, a play workbench, blocks. These children wanted for nothing. In the center of the rug, with a sort of cloth doughnut wrapped around him, sat the baby, who was very intently examining a yellow cube. "Willie-bee," his mother crooned, "look who's here! Your grandpa, come to see you." She went over and scooped him up, and he settled into her arm like a puzzle piece. "Looky, Willie-bee! Say hello." And the child looked at Paul and smiled a gummy smile.

Paul felt himself dazzled. He put his hands, still holding the toy bag, behind his back—what if Jennifer offered the baby to him? In compensation, he leaned forward. "Hello there," he said. He felt the bag hanging against his calf. "I've brought something for you," he said. Oh, the train. His heart pinched again. "For you and your brother." He set the bag on the kitchen counter, realized the box was not gift-wrapped. Well, so much the better. He drew the box out of the bag and held it before the baby's eyes. "Look here!"

"Oh, my," Jennifer said. "How wonderful. Jonathan will *love* it."

Paul wagged the box in front of the baby. "I'll bet your brother will share with you," he said. He wanted so badly to give something to the child.

But Jennifer eased it out of Paul's hands and placed it back in the bag, still holding Willie on her hip. Willie watched with interest. "Oh, we'll save it, won't we, Willie? It has a lot of little pieces that you would just love to put in your mouth." She smiled at Paul. "A good thing he's so little. In a few months he'll be screaming for it."

"Yes, well." Paul put his empty hands in his pockets. "When will Jonathan be back?"

"After lunch, I'm afraid. Can you stay? Why don't I fix you something?"

"Well." He felt unexpectedly free. Cookie had no idea where he was. He was an independent agent. "I'll have some soup, if you've got it."

"Soup?" Jennifer frowned. "My goodness. In this heat. Let me see what I can find."

She rummaged in the pantry; no soup. Could she make him something else? A sandwich? Paul dug in his heels. No need to change his routine. No, nothing. He'd have to leave soon.

"Oh, can't you stay?" He couldn't tell if she was sincere or not. She wanted to hear about the Italy trip; they were leaving tomorrow? She and Teddy had had no idea. So he wouldn't be in Maine. They had already gone in July, she and Teddy, but they were heading up again next week. "And you enjoyed Rhode Island, I'm sure," she said politely.

Cookie had a place down in Narragansett, and Paul now went there with her for the month of July. He did not regret this change in his summer routine, just as he did not regret any changes Cookie had made in his life. The long Maine summers of his children's childhoods seemed very distant, and when he was in Maine (where he would ordinarily be in August, but for Italy), parties with his old tennis partners and fellow cocktail-drinkers seemed more like college reunions, with people whose youth he had shared in a faraway dream, instead of real, ongoing life. His children said they missed him in Maine. He was not sure this was true.

But the thought made him consent to a cup of tea. It was Willie's lunchtime too, and Paul sat at the kitchen table and watched Jennifer spackle orange goo from a small jar into his mouth. It was hard to resist glancing at his watch. Just as he had decided he would make his move, however, the phone rang, and Jennifer went to answer it. "Oh, no," he heard her say. "Poor little guy." She hung up, and then, oddly, kept her back to Paul for an extra moment. "Hmp," she murmured, and then turned to him with a quizzical expression that brightened as she spoke.

"Jonathan's little friend has gotten sick," she said. "Throwing up. So I have to go get him early. Of course, this way he'll get to see you. The thing is"—he felt himself tense—"if I take Willie with me, he might fall asleep in the car. And that would be disastrous. Because then Jonathan would wake him up, and there goes the nap!" Paul smiled weakly. "But I could leave Willie here. It wouldn't be for long."

"Oh, now, I don't think—"

"He's good as gold," Jennifer said, taking the baby out of his chair. "He'll just sit here on the floor and play." She walked over to the rug and set him down, demonstrating. "In a few months it'll be a different story. He'll be crawling all over the place." She seemed to be implying that this was Paul's best, his only chance. "He's not going to poop"—she smiled as Paul blanched—"he did that right before you got here. He's been fed. Really, you can just get to know each other. I'll be back in half an hour. Less."

Jennifer could be pushy. He'd always known that. Not pushy—insistent. But there was a quality to her insistence, a clarity—he had admired it before—she usually did not insist on a bad idea. He tried to quell his panic. She seemed to know what she was doing; it seemed important to her. "All right, dear," he said. "If you think it best."

"Oh, that's wonderful!" She leaned down to Willie and cupped the back of his round little head in her hand, stroked his yellow fuzz with an absolutely sensual gesture. "I love you, baby." She turned to Paul, her face still tender. "Thank you so much."

Perhaps she was right. Perhaps Willie was at an ideal age. He didn't blink when his mother disappeared and the back door slammed. When he finally looked up at Paul, with his watery smile, Paul wondered if it actually did matter if he was there, if the baby would register his presence in any meaningful way at all. Paul looked around at the toys. There were some plastic stacking rings, low-rent cousins of the bright rings of the unpurchased train. He leaned down and dumped them in front of the baby and set the plastic spindle beside them. Willie regarded them solemnly, and then reached for one with a wavering hand. But Paul had placed them too far away, and when the baby reached he collapsed from the middle, stuck with his face on the rug.

Paul watched him, alarmed. Couldn't he get up? Apparently not. The baby, folded in half, started to whimper. This would not do. Paul bent his good knee and, by holding on to the nearby coffee table, was able to ease himself down to the floor. He propped the baby up inside his doughnut cushion. Clever thing, that. Paul was surprised at how small and soft the baby felt, how Paul's hands could span his spongy little middle. He seemed made of a wholly different substance from Paul himself, from Cookie, sinewy and aged. When he was propped, Willie made a satisfied noise. Paul handed him the green ring and he took it, with an underwater motion, his fingers wrapping one by one, careful as a watchmaker. Paul shoved the spindle near. The baby batted at it with the ring, and completely by chance managed to hook it; he took his accomplishment in stride, however, and looked around with a purposeful air. Paul handed him another ring.

He hoped he was doing the right thing. He cleared his throat and said, "Willie, I'm your grandfather." Willie ignored him. "William," Paul said experimentally. "Bill." His father had been Bill. Had his father ever sat on the floor and played with him, Paul, like this? He had honestly never thought about it before. It seemed irrelevant; he would not remember if he had, just as Willie would not remember this day; but all at once Paul wished very hard that he could know for certain. His father had not been a playful man, although no less so than Paul himself. Had his father brought him toys? "Willie," Paul said softly, "I'm going to get you a train. It's a lovely thing, this train." Willie looked up at him. He had not yet hooked the second ring, and instead put it in his mouth. A long silver thread of saliva descended from his lower lip and landed in a jewellike drop on the carpet. "Willie," Paul said sternly. He meant it only in fun. But the baby took the ring out of his mouth, gave Paul a look of betrayal, and began to cry. "Oh, now, Willie," Paul said, in a more sympathetic tone, but the baby rubbed his eyes and cried harder. Bringing his hands to his face threw him off balance, and he collapsed again, this time to the side, so that he was draped over the doughnut. He thrashed around and managed to get onto his back, but now he was stuck like a beetle, his arms and legs waving helplessly in the air.

Paul reached out to sit him up and saw him rub his eyes again. Why, the child was tired! For a moment he felt ridiculously proud of his deduction. Well, he would put the child in his crib. What was so difficult about that? He would find it, somewhere upstairs. The child would go to sleep and Jennifer would come back to an orderly, serene house; then he would leave, fully vindicated, and go home to his soup. He reached forward and picked Willie up. The baby's crying abated somewhat and Paul felt another surge of confidence. Now—to rise himself. He held the baby around the stomach, facing out, with his left arm, and reached for the coffee table with his right. The knee did not seem to be bending very well. He got his other leg under him and held the edge of the table harder. If he pivoted forward, he would be able to get up on the bum leg too. He pulled; went forward more quickly than he had intended; and with a sickening *thwack* the baby's head hit the table.

After an endless, outraged intake of breath, Willie began to howl. "Oh, Jesus," Paul said. There was no blood, but the baby's face was so red Paul thought he might be having cardiac arrest. "Oh, Willie. Oh, Willie." He held him with both arms. At least they were upright now. Motion seemed to be called for. He swayed back and forth. Still the baby cried. He bounced. That seemed to be better. The baby's face was still red, and Paul remembered, from the deep past, that Jean had called such times "the cardiac cry." One of them did it particularly often. Was it Rob, their middle? Yes, it was coming back. Paul held the baby as well as he could and bounced. They had all lived, hadn't they? His four children? Cardiac cries and all?

But still Willie cried, his outrage turning to an elemental sorrow. Paul began to walk. Then walk and bounce. "Yes, love, be quiet," Paul said. "Little Willie. There you go." He still felt strange talking out loud, resisted the urge to look around and assure himself that no one was watching. Walking. Dr. Harris had said to walk a great deal, at this point the knee needed gentle exercise. Too hot to walk outside; if he walked to the front of the house, back to the kitchen, around the island, it made a circuit. "All right, Willie." Back again to the front hall; the dining room needed painting. He had thought Jennifer ran a tight ship. Back to the kitchen. "Now, now." She had said half an hour. When had she left? He didn't know. The baby was quiet. Another circuit. The rhythm of it was good. Dr. Harris might approve of the bouncing too—a gentle bounce. Like the old bounce of the tennis court. Maybe he would get there again. He thought of the clay courts in Fred Sprague's back yard, in Maine, the white light of high summer, just before it turned gold, the *pock* of the ball radiating up his arm, the power of it, how each knee, his whole body, had been an instrument. "Yes, Willie," he said absently, and looked down at the child. His head was drooping. My God, my God—but then Paul realized that he had gone to sleep.

"Well, how about that," Paul whispered. The baby startled, then went limp again. Paul stopped at the foot of the stairs and looked at them doubtfully. Upstairs, somewhere, was the crib; but he realized he would not be able to hold on to the bannister, carrying the child; and what if the knee gave out completely?

He made two more slow tours of the house. He missed his soup. And there was his nap. Suddenly he was exhausted, that delicious peak of afternoon tiredness that meant if he lay down he would be asleep almost immediately. He fought it. What if he dropped the child? Well, he could lie down on the sofa. Put the baby on the chair next to it. Yes, cradle him down where the cushioned back and seat met. There was a smear of something that looked like peanut butter on the chair's arm. He leaned down to place the baby and a thought emerged from the dim, cardiac-cry reaches of his memory—did they stay asleep if you put them down? Sometimes they woke right up. His tiredness now was like vertigo.

All at once he remembered Jean, a very clear picture, Jean and an infant lying on a sofa, both asleep, the baby's head right under Jean's chin. They had been curled together like one organism. Who had it been? Marian? Rob? Teddy? Or little Paul, Paul junior, their first and most miraculous—Paul whom he never saw anymore—Portland, Oregon—what sort of a place was that to move to? Most likely it had been Paul. For after that, how would Jean have been able to lie down, so peacefully, with only one baby in her charge? She had been good at it, Jean had. The babies. The kids. They had not been his concern, not the dailiness of them, their cries and diapers and skinned knees, the weight of them like the weight of this little Willie, the softness of his hair, the defenseless droop of his sleeping head. He remembered seeing Jean like that, with little Paul, and how suddenly moved he had been, caught in a different kind of vertigo, how his love had been so overwhelming that he could do nothing but tip-toe out of the room and leave them alone.

He turned Willie around from his sack-of-potatoes position so they were chest to chest, and sat down on the edge of the sofa. There was a pillow, the perfect size and loft for his head; yes, there. The bum leg went up, then the good one. His shoes were still on; well, there was nothing to be done. Willie was surprisingly heavy. When they were horizontal, the baby burrowed a bit and then was still again, his breathing quiet and regular. Paul curved his arms around the baby's cushioned bottom. His head fit under Paul's chin. Yes, a good solution. Jennifer—was it Jennifer?—would be home soon. He felt himself falling, falling, falling.

There was great hilarity at the Baldwins' that night about how he had spent his afternoon. Somehow, he and Willie had slept on the sofa together for three hours. "I didn't want to wake you," Jennifer had said, when he finally did stir, disoriented, a little nauseated, Willie rustling under his chin with an insistent swimming motion, Paul's shirt damp from their perspiration. Jennifer was standing over them, her face alight, soft. "You were sleeping so soundly. Both of you."

Of course Paul had had to call Cookie, who by that point was frantic with worry and, he suspected, annoyance. In the kitchen, Willie on her shoulder, Jennifer had taken in his end of the conversation, all his assurances and apologies; for some reason he hadn't left the room, as he could have with the cordless phone. And then a most extraordinary thing had happened. Gently, Jennifer removed the phone from his hand and talked Cookie down. "Of course I would have called if I had known," she had said. And then, "I assumed he was in charge of his own schedule."

Paul walked over and sat down with Jonathan, who, big-eyed, was examining his new earthmover. Silently, Paul handed him a construction man, and Jonathan (who was turning four) said, "Fank you," not looking at him, and placed the man inside the cab. Behind them, Jennifer was saying, with a kind but ironclad firmness, "He was visiting his grandson. If you could have seen them, you wouldn't have woken them up either." Pause. "Well, my belief is that if you're sleeping, it's because you need it." A longer pause. "Yes, you too. I hope you have a good trip."

By the time he got home, Cookie had decided his little escapade— this was how she referred to it—was charming. By the time they reached the Baldwins' (she had packed without him), the story was fully formed. "Sleeping right here," Cookie said, patting her chest, as if she had seen it herself. "One of the best naps you ever had, right, dear?"

"Yes, it was." He did not repeat what Jennifer had said that afternoon, as he had stood in the kitchen, dizzy in the bright afternoon light. "Willie will remember this," she had said. "There's a place for memories like this. In your core. This afternoon will always be a part of him."

The dinner party broke up early; Cookie said they needed their rest—"or at least I do, dear. Your tank is full," she said, and everyone laughed again, Henry Baldwin with that enormous booming laugh that made Paul think he never really listened, as if Paul's Willie-nap had been some youthful, jumping-in-a-fountain sort of prank. At home, Cookie performed her swift bathroom routine—swipe of cold cream, blur of toothbrushing—and got straight in bed. "Don't stay up too long," she said. "Long naps aren't REM sleep, you know. Not quality."

"All right. Good night, dear." He stood at her side of the bed, leaned over and gave her a kiss, as if he were tucking her in. Before he had left the room, she had snapped off the light.

He wandered downstairs, feeling adrift. Usually he was in bed first. The kitchen was dark, appliances faintly humming; the set alarm by the front door blinked red. The only light he could find still on was in the living room, the lamp that stood next to his reading chair. The chair itself was new, or at least unfamiliar, whether of his or Cookie's lineage he couldn't remember, and recently reupholstered. But the lamp was old, he knew that, it was attached to a little table, a lamp from the house in Belmont, his and Jean's house. He sat down in the chair, in the yellow pool of light. That had been a big barn of a house. Had to be, to hold all of them, his children, his towering sons, their friends, always exuding a faint odor of sweat, as if they had just come from a playing field—which they usually had. Big enough, too, to hold the dining room table where they would all fit, the refridge with their endless gallons of milk, the stove that produced piles of spaghetti and parades of roast chickens and mountains of rice— and Jean in the middle of it all. Jean. What pictures did he have? Of Jean, of his children? Were there any baby pictures set about? Any Willies of yore?

He stood up and made a quick inspection of the room, all the shelves and tables and desktops. No. In all of these pictures—Rob in his baseball uniform, Marian graduating from Winsor, young Paul and Teddy on the beach—his children were older, evinced some hint, more, of who they were to become. Cookie liked having the pictures of his family out. She liked the fact of his family, accepted it unquestioningly. Yes, she had accepted a great deal. But there were no pictures of Jean. He did not remember retiring them for Cookie's benefit, but he must have. Would she care? Did Cookie know that there had been a completeness to his life then, a heady busyness, before any child had grown up and left—that they had been a unit unto themselves, no appendages, no gaps, the past and present and future all balanced and bright? He sat down again in his reading chair. Ah, Jean. He had not expected this, the hot streaming tears, how momentarily alien this room felt, the room of his new beginning. Jean would understand. The tears, and why he shed them so infrequently, and where he was now. She wouldn't fault him for it.

He wiped his eyes with his pajama sleeve and imagined the room thronged with pictures, Jean, his babies, Cookie too, his parents. He imagined all his own memories, the unseen ones that held him up, like buried stones of a foundation, plastered-over oak beams. Who had held him as a baby? His mother, dark-haired, with her little humming songs? Had Mamie, still practically a baby herself, stroked his cheek, had they looked at each other with clear, unremembering eyes? And his father—he knew now that his father had brought him toys. A train, going around and around. Yes, he could see the house, the white farmhouse with the orange trees coming right up to the yard, could feel the relentless heat and the mosquitoes, saw the inside neat and dim, himself in the living room, on the round rag rug, next to the corner cupboard, his father beside him. Was not himself but saw himself, as if passing by a plate glass window, the scene confused with his reflection; but his movement was inexorable, and the picture shrank, wavered and vanished.

He had left Florida too soon, too thoughtlessly. He knew that too. He had wanted the life his father had rejected, the life he had sensed was superior, the life, indeed, he now had, of books and ideas and the symphony and the university and all these things that had had weight long before he arrived, and would after he was gone. Yes, he knew he had left too easily, too eagerly, but he knew also that his mother and father and even Mamie had forgiven him by now.

And Jean? The children? Had they forgiven him all his faults, his lacks, his omissions? He did not think his roster of sins was any longer than the next man's. Or any shorter. Well.

He got up from the chair, his knee needing oil, and switched off the lamp. The room went dark, but not as dark as he had expected; cold light flooded in from the window, and as his eyes adjusted the whole room melded into a photographic black and white. He went to the window. High above, the moon was fiercely bright. The back garden was silver in its light, the shadows sharp as rulers, colors asleep but the thingness of the things not. The rose arbor at the end of the walk cast a tall, rounded shadow on the grass (of which every blade seemed visible) that was clearer than it would have been on a cloudless afternoon. He could almost make out the thorns. How could this be? How was it that now, at seventy-eight, he was seeing the brightest moonlight of his life? He stood at the window, wondering. And he realized he was going to die.

He had thought about death before, of course, many times. He had thought about it in 1943 in particular, with Fred Sprague beside him at Mignano, and also that blond, blue-eyed boy from Nebraska who had seemed a prime poetic candidate to get his brains shot out before Paul's eyes; but he had not, had survived as well as Paul and Fred, and still sent Christmas cards. Paul had been terrified then, had looked death in the face and not liked what he saw, but he had had no premonitions. Now, however, he knew quite simply that his time would soon be over. He wondered when it would be. Hopefully not in Rome. What a burden for poor Cookie. Yes, Cookie. He thought of her upstairs, sleeping her well-earned sleep, and felt boundless gratitude. He would be sorry to leave her.

He turned away from the window and the room seemed ordinary again, still a little ghostly but the furniture seemed right, the pictures, whatever their number. It was where he was now; it was his life. Paul knew it was possible to be nostalgic for anything, as long as it was in the past. Look at John Andersson, from Nebraska, and even Fred, sentimental about the war. So many of them were. So many deaths then—but he had made it this far.

He went back to the hallway and slowly climbed the stairs. He barely noticed the knee; he knew that it was a temporary inconvenience. Ah, Cookie, down the hall, Jean, waiting for him, if one could indulge in a bit of religious romanticism. And little Willie?—out in Belmont, safe in his crib, small limbs flung wide in the hot night—Willie he would have to leave, for now. The weight of that baby on his chest. Something he would have liked to give Cookie, in another life. But there was only one life to think about now. One line. One beginning, one middle, one end. Where had this come from? This knowledge? This moonlight? A shift of mere seconds. Now he felt a little dazed. But stronger than he would have expected. Yes, quite strong. The house, this particular house, all the houses, all of his time, cradled him in endless arms, and when the falling began, or whether, in fact, it was flying, he could not say. ✧

# Flap

Rick Moody

The thing is that I've developed this flap of skin on my wrist. I think it was after the argument with Leslie, where she was saying that anti-bacterial soap didn't do any good. I get passionate about things. I know I had to get up really early one morning, and right when the alarm was screeching I was having a nightmare about postal delivery. There was a part about some entity reaching up from the interior of the mailbox and grabbing my arm and pulling me down. When I woke up, I remember seeing the flap. Not a little flap, either. More like a gill. Like I have a gill on my wrist. I didn't panic, you know, I didn't think, well, this must be some kind of dangerous medical condition. This is kind of embarrassing, but the first thing I thought was that the flap might be a sort of vaginal flap. I consider myself one of those guys who's always had a certain amount of vagina envy. I mean, I think vaginas are pretty. So my first thought was: maybe I had developed this flap through some kind of vagina envy. Maybe if I had a vagina I could know more about them. On the other hand, it's true that I did quit therapy after the session where my counselor fell asleep, and sure this experience made me skeptical about therapy and about the kind of ideas you might spend your money on in therapy. I wasn't sure if the vagina theory wasn't just, you know, a first take on the issue. If I'd been smart, I would have just *felt* up the flap, to see if there was anything clitoral up there. If it were a vagina, there would have been a clitoris there somewhere, right? I mean, I don't always know where the clitoris is, but if I felt a little shiver that would be a pretty good sign that I had a flap and a clitoris on my wrist. On the other hand, you know, maybe the flap was a wound, even though I couldn't remember anything like that. A slash of some kind. Some barely healed wound. Guys often think this about vaginas when they are young and naive, that vaginas are wounds. Also, I read about the Salem Witch Trials one time, and apparently the witches in Salem, used to get right up next to people's beds, and, while these people were sleeping, the witches would *bite* them. Just sink in their front teeth. So maybe I was being slashed in my sleep. Maybe there was some witch getting right up next to my bed at night. Maybe Leslie was slashing me. Because of the argument about anti-bacterial soap. Maybe my girlfriend was a witch. She had a pretty awesome pair of scissors in her desk drawer. And her teeth were in good shape. It'd be easy to slash me. At night I'm pretty trusting. I sleep hard for the first few hours, any given night. Maybe my girlfriend was a witch, and I was slashed at night, around eleven or so, and I was bleeding, and the flap was a wound. It'd be a pretty compelling theory, you have to admit, except for the fact that I wasn't bleeding. The flap was getting bigger, but it wasn't bleeding.

I needed to go to the post office. For stamps. I know a guy there. Mitch. Mitch says it's a good job. The pension is great. I was trying to buy some of those new Stars of Hollywood stamps. I forked over a twenty, asked for stamps featuring the guy from *North by Northwest*, chased by a crop duster, when Mitch said, astounded, "That is some flap you got." Looked like my skin was unwinding. I was seeing it from the other side of the service window, through Mitch's eyes. Mitch was in the middle of counting back. He was agape. My skin was a bandage, and it was unwinding, and whatever was underneath there was going to show through. And what was underneath? Wiring? Sheet rock? Asbestos?

Later that evening: I had to get my kid from my ex-wife's place. It was my night with the kid. On the way over, I noticed that my flap was actually flapping in the breeze. Like it was a little prayer flag. Or a pennant. My flap was saluting the breezes. Definitely some part of my body was coming off. In middle age, all the surfaces start coming off. Like you're moulting a layer. Like aluminum siding is shearing off of you. My daughter noticed right away. My daughter said I looked like I was made of wet cardboard. She wouldn't hug me at first. She stood in the center of the living room, by the coffee table, arms crossed, like she never wanted to cooperate with visitation again. I didn't care. I was daydreaming. And what I was day- dreaming about was my flap. Maybe I liked it a little bit. I was thinking maybe my flap was an actual flap, like *flap A*, which needed to be put in *slot B* somewhere. You know? Like with those instruction manuals that come with complicated gifts. I was an envelope, basically. Standing in my ex-wife's living room. And my daughter was crying, and saying she didn't want to go with me. I was too weird, my daughter said. However, an incontrovertible fact was about to emerge. My ex-wife had *places to go*, nails to be manicured, and she wasn't going to get into any discussion. Visitation would take place, without interruption. I said to my daughter, "So what if I have a flap? I'm still your dad."

I was driving her toward the fast food joint next to the aquarium, and I got this idea that maybe my flap was more like a flipper. Maybe my flap was pre-historic somehow. Atavistic. I was doing a lot of theorizing. That's just how it was going to go. I was a dolphin or a manatee. I was a guy with an ancient aquatic flipper, the kind of flipper on a mammal that lurched up out of a muddy swamp and onto dry land where grubs and insects were more plentiful. I was going down through evolutionary history, like in that William Hurt movie. I was going to be one of those amphibious mammals, and then maybe after that I would be a giant squid, and then a jellyfish. This would be interesting. Although it was true that there were lots of people who could make something more important out of turning into a jellyfish, like one of the experts at the aquarium, or maybe a per- formance artist, like that guy who wanted to have an extra ear grafted onto his arm. I was the divorced owner of a successful chain of car wash- es. Not first choice for a guy who should be an evolutionary miracle. I was kind of a fuckup, in fact. I couldn't even get Leslie to let me move in with her. I had messed up more things than a lot of people I knew. Maybe the flap was a curse. Maybe my flap was some biological tendency that had been triggered after I cheated at golf two weeks ago. I never should have lied about three-putting. I could tell that Mitch's brother-in-law knew. I'm a blusher. There was also the lie I told Leslie about having flirted with that nineteen-year-old after some drinks at the Chinese place last month. Nineteen? After a certain point, the girl just walked away, probably, because I'm old and I have a kid, and I owe massive child support, and the loans on my business are crushing me.

That reminds me. My company operates best in a climate of respect. I treat the guys who work for me with respect. But it's hard to meet your employees on the level playing field when your arm looks like it was borrowed from the *Mummy* costume shop. Everyone around the car washes has skin ailments. It's hard. From the water and the cleaning agents. That's why I keep on *believing* where anti-bacterial soap is concerned. On Thursday, everyone at the office wanted to believe that the flap had to do with this stuff. Pete Bowes, one of the guys on the line downtown, asked me if I wanted him just to cut off the flap. He had a really good pocket knife with him. Natch, I'd considered going to one of the many cosmetic surgeons here in the Miami-Dade area, but I don't really trust surgeons, they're all about cutting, never about rapport, so I decided, why the hell not, why not Pete, as long as he sterilized properly. I had a few snorts from the desk flask, and he cut off as much of the flap he could get. I promoted him to ass't manager on the spot.

Next day, it was back. If anything, a little bigger and more infected than it had been before. You know how those cylinders of dinner rolls look when you first pop them out of the container. My arm looked like that. I wanted to butter myself. There was no way around it. I had to go see, Arnold Piccolo, M.D. I'd known the guy in high school, when he was a teenaged alcoholic. He'd long since cleaned up, and his office had that isopropyl smell. Problem was, I think maybe Arnie had some kind of nerve damage from all the drinking. He had this tic where it seemed like he was looking over at his shoulder. He'd do it a couple of times every sentence. It was like he'd sprouted an additional eye on his shoulder and he wanted to make eye contact. He seemed to be having trouble concentrating, which would be natural if you had to look over your shoulder that often. "Arnie," I said, "Can you tell me what this is?" I whipped off the suede glove I'd taken to wearing. Arnie managed to get the tic under control long enough to give me the once over. He probed at the diaphanous sheets of flesh coming off. There was a silence. He put some of the skin under a cheap microscope. While he was looking he said, "Look, I gotta ask, do you ever think about those days?" And I said, "Which days?" Like I didn't know. Jesus. Arnie said, "Those days." He was pushing the tissue sample around under the microscope. I said, "Arnie, once I was quick-witted, once I carried a six-pack on my person, once I could charm any girl on the beach out of blouse, once I could surf a little bit, and once I could open a beer bottle with my teeth, but now Arnie, I'm kind of too busy for this kind of standard-issue nostalgic conversation, because time is money, Arnie, for you and me both, and the whole top layer of my body is coming unglued, and I need to get to the bottom of it." Arnie said he needed to run more tests. Of course, I was still out ten bucks of co-pay.

I never even called him back. I was bored of explaining. I was bored of making bad jokes. *Hey, I'm trying to get work as a mail slot.* Never mind about the weird moisture that started coursing out of the warm, clammy space under the flap from thumb joint to elbow. It had a salty taste, not poisonous. Like tear juice. Could have been salivary, I figured. Okay, I did try one more thing, I tried *feeding* the flap. I could stuff something nutritive in there, I figured, as long as it came from the health food store, and if the flap wanted to ingest whatever I put in it, then I'd see that the flap was actually another mouth. Kind of creepy, I know, but not that horrible. I mean, I do like to eat. I was having sushi in town, even though I don't really eat the raw fish anymore, what with the microbes. And I just shoved the roll with the fish roe in under the flap. I never eat the roe anyway. Too fishy. I shoved it under the flap, while Leslie was telling me about the affair her boss was having, and immediately the flap gobbled up the sushi roll. It was the weirdest sensation. I mean, I just should not have a throat in my wrist, especially since I'm right-handed. What if there was a choking incident? Leslie said, "Jesus, Ed, did your wrist just eat that sushi roll? You don't even like roe!" The enormity of my situation began to sink in. "Do you think it has its own stomach or something? Or another esophagus?"

Did I say this already? I always thought Leslie was too beautiful for me. And too young. I always thought she'd realize that I wasn't good enough, because I'd had my adventures, like I was telling Arnie that day. I'd hung out in the parking lots before concerts, tailgating in the company of people with dreadlocks. I'd done all that stuff when I was young, but now I just needed to make the child support payments. Leslie didn't want to spend the rest of her life with a guy who owned a car wash business. She'd get to a point where she'd just say that she had a prior engagement. Leslie was in possession of the facts: I was bald, old, didn't want my workers to unionize, I was obsessed with hygiene. All these worries were like a chorus yelling in my head, so much that at first I didn't hear it. Didn't hear it at first because I thought it was coming from the next table. I thought I was listening to someone really irritating at the next table. But it wasn't the next table, because there was no one at the next table. It wasn't Leslie doing some ventriloquist routine. It wasn't me. The maitre d' was a young Japanese woman romancing the sushi chef across the room. That left only one possibility. *The flap had started talking.* Right at the table, like it was going to seize control of the situation. The flap had a bit of a lisp. Which was sort of embarrassing. I mean, my flap should have had a virile, masculine voice. But it did turn out to be a strong persuader. It wouldn't give up. And the biggest difference between me and the flap was that the flap *believed* in me, even if I didn't believe in myself. And here's what it said. It said to Leslie, "What are you waiting for, honey? Are you waiting for Mr. Perfect? Because if you're waiting for Mr. Perfect, you're going to be waiting a long time! This fella here loves you! And he may have some flaws, but those flaws are only *skin deep*! This guy loves to be loved, and he loves to give the gift of love! He loves the gift of giving! And he's neat and he picks up after himself, and I personally have seen him empty the garbage can without even being asked! Plus, he's a successful business owner. So if you're just waiting for the better thing to come along, you're going to wait a long time! You should try to see the beauty that's underneath the surfaces, because that's the beauty that lasts. Not that you need my advice—" The flap said *advice* like it rhymed with *scythe*. And it spit food. Talked with its mouth full. It was definitely a free spirit, if a little bit sloppy. And it sure was sentimental. Still, I was personally moved to tears by the flap's defense. Even more so when Leslie pulled me close. And reached into her pocketbook for the anti-bacterial wipes.  ✧

# Travelogue

Vincent Standley

I quit the camera store after three weeks, then stayed at Judy's, running errands, making her coffee, mostly trying to keep out of the way. I'd been there for a month like that when she told me to get lost.

My last paycheck went for an economy flight to England, with a layover in some place I'd never heard of. The weather in London was really, really, shitty cold. And there was this guy, a friend of Judy's, I can't remember his name, but he was a cartoonist. His name and address were written on a scrap piece of paper Judy had stuck inside my ticket envelope.

From London, and following directions from strangers, I walked across the river there, and then if you walk all day you finally come to where this guy's town is, this cartoonist, but, before that, when I first arrived in London, I had a cold, so I stayed at a B and B, which is like a house except it's a hotel, for two days. I bought lozenges and hid out eating canned beef from a can.

It was nightfall before I got there to this guy's house, but nobody was there. And it was dark, and I didn't feel like spending another night at another B and B, so I went to a pub with a hanging sign of an elephant and drank beer and talked with the bartender. You'll be fine, laddy, he said. Have another jar.

Incidentally, this happened again when I visited New York City and I caught the last ferry to Staten Island, because I had remembered hearing about it when I was a kid, but being winter it was off-season, and the hotels and restaurants were all closed, so I sat inside a bar till two o'clock in the morning. The bartender asked me what I was doing, and I told him I had no place to go, so he let me sleep in the cab of his truck with blankets soaked in engine oil.

I found myself a day's walk from London, then, rehearsing what's to come, drinking and sitting with strangers trying not to look too nervous or outsiderish. After the beer, I knocked a second time at the guy's door. At any rate, not only was his mom there but her boyfriend too, and they were expecting me. They'd gotten a call from Judy who'd told them I'd be coming. It was a relief to feel welcome somewhere. They made me tea, and I got sobered up, and then, eventually, this cartoonist came home, and we all had a good time playing dominos.

The next day Judy's friend took me out on the town, to London, where we went busking, playing punk songs on an acoustic guitar so they sounded like folk songs, and all day moving back and forth from the street to the subway station from Piccadilly Circus to Leicester Square to Victoria Station and other places. By late afternoon we had a pile of money, and the cartoonist bought me lunch, where we had whitefish and bread.

There are squats there—free rooms for squatters, whole complexes of squats for people to sleep in. And it all seems perfectly legal, and that's where this guy stayed when he was in the city. He had a pretty nice place, a blue room, which they called the Blue Room, and I wondered why I hadn't gone there first thing instead of walking all day getting lost after crossing the Thames river and passing the airport and everything. There was a bathtub. They had electricity, and there were other people staying there. One guy was from Scotland and the guy down the hall was from Scotland too, and a girl named Genie, a kind of lethargic, dominatrix type. So she sat back and dug into her leather purse and contemplated whether she wanted chips or beer or hash or cider, and everyone seemed to have money, but none of them could decide if they wanted chips or beer or hash or cider. They had a TV, and there were parties just like our parties, and everyone was drunk by nine p.m., but you couldn't understand anyone because it was just party noise with an English accent.

There were Dutch Hells Angels. They were fat but somehow also into speed. They had just come over from Amsterdam, where they had bought it, which gave me the idea to go to Amsterdam too.

But the next day I took a trip down to Brighton. I think I was lonely. The nice thing about Brighton was there were some girls there who seemed interested in me. One said she liked my nose. I could've stayed in Brighton, but there was a bug in my ear for Amsterdam, so I took a train, then a boat, and then another train.

I shot up in the train station with a hypodermic needle meant for horses. It was large and plastic, propped between my knees, sticking in my vein. The stuff was supposed to be heroin but wasn't, and I spent two days and nights sick in the hostel bathroom, my arm swollen glossy-blue.

The hostel in Amsterdam is high-tech with metal stairs and a PA system with loud speakers for announcements. It has a bar that attracts teenagers from New Zealand who travel around the world for years before going back to their island. The place was so nice it made me sicker than the heroin, so I left there early the third morning, landing in the red light district by noon. A prostitute sold me a pile of speed or cocaine. By this time the rig was lost, so I ate the stuff, and for ten hours sat cross-legged in the middle of a frozen canal drawing ducks with a pencil and a broken piece of crayon.

When you leave Amsterdam for England, you take a train to the dock where I was strip searched, and the film container which they didn't check with the hash in it I accidentally put on the table, and, then, when they checked my pockets, I had the one I thought had the hash in it, but it really had my spare change, so by sheer luck I ended up getting through without getting caught, and shared my hash with Judy's friend back at the Blue Room.

I was arrested and spent five days in jail hoping they'd deport me. By the time I was out, someone had stolen my clothes, so the cops gave me new ones. I stepped out of the municipal precinct with pegged slacks and an Italian jacket, dressed up like a real mod. I called Judy collect, who said she'd help get me home, but only wired enough cash for a ticket to New York City.

On my last day in London, the cartoonist shaved my head and all the hair off my body, and gave me a pair of blue suede platform shoes, which were uncomfortable, but which I put on anyway and told him thanks for everything before I left.

My first night back in the States I slept on a rooftop in Greenwich Village, and in the morning I had blisters on my feet. I spent a few hours spare changing, got enough to buy food and walked around the rest of the day getting lost. By nightfall I was limping and freezing cold in the Mod clothes and those shoes making me taller than usual, which was nothing compared to the prostitutes in Times Square, who were nearly naked, walking the avenue in spiked heels, breath trailing past bare shoulders. None of them looked very happy, and I watched a girl shit inside a hotel doorway, another vomit in the street, unfazed by the stuff on her clothes and the traffic she blocked—honking horns—just not responding. I returned to my sleeping bag on the roof and masturbated with the mayonnaise from a take-out order.

I went to Port Authority and snuck on a Greyhound to San Francisco, which broke down in Pennsylvania when a wheel fell off. In Chicago it became known that I had no ticket, and I had to hitchhike the rest of the way back to S.F.

From the Waterfront, where I got dropped off, I walked to Judy's flat on 14th and Bartlett, and she had a pile of Quaaludes and was calling other dealers trying to line up a trade for something else. I said it didn't matter what we did as long as she wasn't on the phone all night, which started her yelling at me, and she called me a hick. Then pretty soon it's the middle of the night, and I'm outside with my duffel bag and no shoes on.

I pace that short block on Bartlett Street between 13th and 14th figuring that eventually she'd come looking for me. I walk back and forth, trying to keep warm, and when you think about it, London and San Francisco are similar in the winter, and my feet are getting wet and numb and picking up tiny pebbles from the sidewalk. I sit down on the curb, using the duffel bag as a cushion, sitting cross-legged and hugging myself from the cold.

Because it is the Mission District and I am alone, because I am white and because my back is exposed, they attack from behind. Five Mexican kids. My legs and arms like rubber from the 'ludes, and I don't feel much but helpless and panicked in a way that's worse than all their punches. I curl up in a ball, moving my hands back and forth between my face and nuts, using the duffel bag as a shield, buried in kicks and punches and yells that don't make any sense to me. Those street lights on Bartlett are spaced about a block apart, and I watch the shadows break up with the sound into echoes, like two smaller screens or a big one split down the middle, and up pulls this Austin Healy sports car. My face is ground into the gravel and tarmac, and I'm talking to these guys, but for some reason, I can see them as clear as day. They speak with English accents; they wear ascots and leather pilot's hats.

I say, what's going on here? they ask.

I'm being pummeled.

Pommeled?

Pummeled! I say.

We've got to help the poor chap! they say.

The Austin Healy is a life-size model of a sports car, which I grab hold of by the spare wheel attached to the trunk and we drive away. There's a density to the road, though it appears in grainy color. We head toward Noe Valley. I keep yelling at them. We pass the Church Street Station. The Cholos disappear. They disappear around the corner, and there's humming and walking, and feet scuff as someone passes. I crawl toward Judy's door. She's a place to go. If I look up it will ruin everything.  ✧

# The Smile on Happy Chang's Face

Tom Perrotta

The Superior Wallcoverings Wildcats were playing in the Little League championship game, and I wanted them to lose. I wanted the Town Pizza Ravens and their star pitcher, Lori Chang, to humiliate them, to run up the score and taunt them mercilessly from the first-base dugout. I know this isn't an admirable thing for a grown man to admit—especially a grown man who has agreed to serve as home-plate umpire—but there are feelings you can't hide from yourself, even if you'd just as soon chop off your hand as admit them to anyone else.

I had nothing against the Wildcat players. It was their coach I didn't like, my next-door neighbor, Carl DiSalvo, the Kitchen Kabinet King of Northern New Jersey. I stood behind the backstop, feeling huge and bloated in my cushiony chest protector, and watched him hit infield practice. A shamelessly vain man, Carl had ripped the sleeves off his sweatshirt, the better to display the rippling muscles he worked for like a dog down at Bally's. I knew all about his rippling muscles. Our driveways were adjacent, and Carl always seemed to be returning from an exhilarating session at the gym just as I was trudging off to work in the morning, my head still foggy from another rotten night's sleep.

"I'm getting pretty buff," he would tell me, proudly rubbing his pecs or biceps. "Wish I'd been built like this when I was younger."

*Fuck you*, I invariably thought, but I always said something polite, like, "Keep it up," or "I gotta start working out myself."

Carl and I had known each other forever. In high school we played football together—I was a starter, a second-team All-County linebacker, while Carl barely dirtied his uniform—and hung out in the same athletic crowd. When he and Marie bought the Detmeyers' house nine years ago, it had seemed like a lucky break for both of us, a chance to renew a friendship that had died of natural causes when we graduated and went our separate ways—me to college and into the management sector, Carl into his father's remodeling business. I helped him with the move, and when we finished, we sat on my patio with our wives, drinking beer and laughing as the summer light faded and our kids played tag on the grass. We called each other "neighbor" and imagined barbecues and block parties stretching far into the future.

"Nice pick-up, Trevor," he called to his third baseman. "But let's keep working on that throw, okay pal?"

So many things had happened since then. I was still living in the same house, but Jeanie and the kids were gone. And I had come to despise Carl, even though he'd done nothing to deserve it except live his own happy life right next to my sad one, where I had no choice but to witness it all the time and pretend not to mind.

*Go fuck yourself,* I thought. *Okay, pal?*

"Jackie *boy.*" Tim Tolbert, the first-base umpire and president of the Little League, pummeled my chest protector as though it were a punching bag. "Championship *game.*" He looked happier than a grown man has a right to be. "*Very* exciting."

As usual, I wanted to grab him by the collar and ask what the hell he had to be so cheerful about. He was a baby-faced, prematurely bald man who sold satellite dishes all day, then came home to his wife, a scrawny exercise freak obsessed with her son's peanut allergy. She'd made a big stink about it when the kid entered kindergarten, and now the school cafeteria wasn't allowed to serve PB&J sandwiches anymore.

"Very exciting," I agreed. "Two best teams in the league."

"Not to mention the two best umps," he said, giving me a brotherly squeeze on the shoulder.

This much I owed to Tim—he was the guy who convinced me to volunteer as an umpire. He must have known how isolated I was feeling, alone in my house, my wife and kids living with my mother-in-law, nothing to do at night but stare at the TV and stuff my face with sandwich cream cookies. I resisted at first, not wanting to give people a new opportunity to whisper about me, but he kept at it until finally I gave in.

And I loved it. Crouching behind the catcher, peering through the horizontal bars of my mask, my whole being focused on the crucial, necessary difference between a ball and a strike, I felt clear-headed and almost serene, free of the bitterness and shame that were my constant companions during the rest of my life.

"Two best umps?" I glanced around in mock confusion. "Me and who else?"

An errant throw rolled against the backstop and Carl jogged over to retrieve it. He grabbed the ball and straightened up, turning to Tim and me as if we'd asked for his opinion.

"Kids are wound tight," he said. "I keep telling 'em it doesn't matter if you win or lose, but I don't think they believe me."

Carl grinned, letting us know he didn't believe it, either. Like me, he was in his mid-forties, but he was carrying it off with a little more panache than I was. He had thick gray hair that made for a striking contrast with his still-youthful body, and a gap between his front teeth that women supposedly found irresistible (at least that's what Jeanie used to tell me). His thick gold necklace glinted in the evening sun, spelling his name to the world.

"You're modeling the proper attitude," Tim told him. "That's all you can do."

The previous fall, a guy named Joe Funkhauser, the father of one of our high school football players, got into an argument with an opposing player's father in the parking lot after a bitterly contested game. Funkhauser beat the guy into a coma, and was later charged with attempted murder. The Funkhauser Incident, as the papers called it, attracted a lot of unfavorable attention to our town, and triggered a painful round of soul-searching among people concerned with youth sports. In response to the crisis, Tim had organized a workshop for Little League coaches and parents, trying to get them to focus on fun rather than competition, but it takes more than a two-hour seminar to change people's attitudes about something as basic as the difference between winning and losing.

"I don't blame your team for being spooked," I said. "Not after what Lori did to them last time. Didn't she set some kind of league record for strikeouts?"

Carl's grin disappeared. "I've been meaning to talk to you about that, Jack. The strike zone's down here. Not up here." He illustrated this point by slicing imaginary lines across his stomach and throat.

"Right," I said. "And it's six points for a touchdown."

"I don't mean to be a jerk about it," he continued, "but I thought you were making some questionable judgments."

"Funny," I said. "They're only questionable when they don't go your way."

"Just watch the high strikes, that's all I'm saying."

Tim kept smiling stiffly throughout this exchange, as if it were all just friendly banter, but he seemed visibly relieved by the sight of Ray Santelli, the Ravens' manager, returning from the snack bar with a hot dog in each hand.

"Just got outta work," he said, by way of explanation. "Traffic was a bitch on the Parkway."

Ray was a dumpy guy with an inexplicably beautiful Russian wife. A lot of people assumed she was mail order, despite Ray's repeated claims that he'd met her at his cousin's wedding. He ran a livery business with his brother, and sometimes kept a white stretch limo parked in the driveway of his modest Cape Cod on Dunellen Street. The car was like the wife, a little too glamorous for its humble surroundings.

"It's those damn toll plazas," observed Tim. "They were supposed to be gone twenty years ago."

Before anyone could chime in with the ritual agreement, our attention was diverted by the appearance of Mikey Fellner wielding his video camera. A mildly retarded guy in his early twenties, Mikey was a familiar figure at local sporting events, graduations, carnivals, and political meetings. He videotaped everything and saved the tapes, which he labeled and shelved in chronological order in his parents' garage. This was apparently part of the syndrome he had—it wasn't Down's but something more exotic, I forget the name—some compulsion to keep everything fanatically organized. He trained the camera on me, then got a few seconds of Santelli wiping mustard off his chin.

"You guys hear?" Carl asked. "Mikey says they're gonna show the game on cable access next week."

Mikey panned over to Tim, holding the camera just a couple of inches from his face. He wasn't big on respecting other people's boundaries, especially when he was working. Tim didn't seem to mind, though.

"Championship *game*," he said, giving a double thumbs-up to the viewing audience. "*Very* exciting."

Little League is a big deal in our town. You could tell that just by looking at our stadium. We've got dugouts, a big electronic scoreboard, and a padded outfield fence covered with ads for local businesses, just like the pro teams (that's how we paid for the scoreboard). We play the national anthem over a really good sound system, nothing like the scratchy loudspeaker they used when I was a kid. The bleachers were packed for the championship game, and not just with the families of the players. It was a bonafide local event.

The Wildcats were up first, and Carl was right: his team had a bad case of the jitters. The leadoff hitter, Justin O'Malley, stepped up to the plate white-knuckled and expecting the worst, as if Lori Chang were Roger Clemens. He planted himself as far away from the plate as possible, stood like a statue for three called strikes, and seemed relieved to return to the bench. The second batter, Mark Rigato, swung blindly at three bad pitches, including a high and tight third strike that almost took his head off. His delayed evasive action, combined with the momentum of his premature swing, caused him to pirouette so violently that he lost his balance and ended up face down in the dirt.

"Strike three," I said, taking care to keep my voice flat and matter-of-fact. I wasn't one of those show-off umps who said *Stee-rike!*, and did a big song and dance behind the plate. "Batter's out."

The words were barely out of my mouth when Carl came bounding out of the third-base dugout. He had his bare arms spread wide, as if volunteering for a crucifixion.

"Goddammit, Jack! That was a beanball!"

I wasn't fooled by his theatrics. By that point, just six pitches into the first inning, it was already clear that Lori Chang was operating at the top of her game, and you didn't need Tim McCarver to tell you that Carl was trying to mess with her head. I should've ordered him back to the dugout and called for play to resume, but there was just enough of a taste in my mouth from our earlier encounter that I took the bait. I removed my mask and took a few steps in his direction.

"Please watch your language, Coach. You know better than that."

"She's throwing at their heads!" Carl was yelling now, for the benefit of the spectators. "She's gonna kill someone!"

"The batter swung," I reminded him.

"He was trying to protect himself. You gotta warn her, Jack. That's your job."

"You do your job, Carl. I'll take care of mine."

I had just pulled my mask back over my head when Tim came jogging across the infield to back me up. We umpires made it a point to present a unified front whenever a dispute arose.

"It's okay," I told him. "Let's play ball."

He gave me one of those subtle headshakes, the kind you wouldn't have noticed if he hadn't been standing six inches in front of you.

"He's right, Jack. You should talk to her."

"You're playing right into his hands."

"Maybe so," he admitted. "But this is the championship. Let's keep it under control."

He was forcing me into an awkward position. I didn't want to be Carl's puppet, but I also didn't want to argue with Tim right there in the middle of the infield. As it was, I could feel my authority draining away by the second. Someone on the Ravens' side yelled for us to stop yapping and get on with the game. A Wildcats fan suggested we'd been bought and paid for by Town Pizza.

"We gotta be careful here." Tim gestured toward the Wildcats' dugout, where Mikey had his video camera set up on a tripod. "This is gonna be on TV."

Lori Chang smiled quizzically as I approached the mound, as if she couldn't possibly imagine why I was paying her a social visit in the middle of the game.

"Is something wrong?" she asked, sounding a little more worried than she looked.

Lori was one of only three girls playing in our Little League that season. I know it's politically incorrect to say so, but the other two, Allie Regan and Steph Murkowski, were tomboys—husky, tough-talking jockettes you could easily imagine playing college rugby and marching in Gay Pride parades later in their lives.

Lori Chang, on the other hand, didn't even look like an athlete. She was petite, with a round, serious face, and lustrous hair that she wore in a ponytail threaded through the back of her baseball cap. Unlike Allie and Steph, both of whom were fully developed in a chunky, none-too-feminine way, Lori had not yet reached puberty. She was lithe and curveless, her chest as flat as a boy's beneath the stretchy fabric of her Ravens jersey. And yet—I hope it's okay for me to talk like this, because it's true—there was something undeniably sexual about her presence on the baseball field. She wore lipstick and nail polish, giggled frequently for no reason, and blushed when her teammates complimented her performance. She was always tugging down her jersey in the back, as if she suspected the shortstop and third baseman of paying a little too much attention to her ass. In short, she was completely adorable. If I'd been twelve, I would've had a hopeless crush on her.

Which is why is it was always such a shock when she let loose with the high, hard one. Unlike other pitchers her age, who struggled just to put the ball over the plate, Lori actually had a strategy, a potent combination of control, misdirection, patience, and outright intimidation. She tended to jam batters early in the count, and occasionally brushed them back, though to my knowledge, she'd never actually hit anyone. Mid-count, she often switched to change-ups and breaking balls, working on the outside corner. Once she had the batter appropriately spooked and thoroughly off-balance, she liked to rear back and finish him off with a sizzler right down the pipe. These two-strike fastballs hopped and dived so unpredictably that it was easy to lose track of them. Some of the batters didn't even realize the ball had crossed the plate until they heard the slap of leather against leather, and turned in angry amazement to see a small but decisive puff of dust rising from the catcher's mitt.

I had no idea where she learned to pitch like that. Lori was a newcomer to our town, one of those high-achieving Asian kids who've flocked here in the past decade (every year, it seems, the valedictorian of our high school has a Chinese or Korean or Indian last name). In just a few months, she'd established herself as an excellent student, a gifted violinist, and a powerhouse on the baseball diamond, despite the fact that she could usually be found waiting tables and filling napkin dispensers at Happy Wok #2, the restaurant her parents had opened on Grand Avenue.

"There's nothing wrong," I told her. "Just keep right on doing what you're doing."

Her eyes narrowed with suspicion. "You came all the way out here to tell me that?"

"It's really not that far," I said, raising my mask just high enough so she could see that I was smiling.

By the end of the third inning, Lori had struck out eight of the first nine batters she'd faced. The only Wildcat to even make contact with the ball was Ricky DiSalvo, Carl's youngest son and the league leader in home runs and RBIs, who got handcuffed by a fastball and dinged a feeble check-swing groundout to second.

Lori's father, Happy Chang, was sitting by himself in the third-base bleachers, surrounded by Wildcats fans. Despite his nickname, Mr. Chang was a grim, unfriendly man who wore the same dirty beige windbreaker no matter how hot or cold it was, and always seemed to need a shave. Unlike the other Asian fathers in our town—most of them were doctors, computer scientists, and businessmen who played golf and made small talk in perfect English—Happy Chang had a rough edge, a just-off-the-boat quality that reminded me of those guys you often saw milling around on Canal Street in the city, making disgusting noises and spitting on the sidewalk. I kept glancing at him as the game progressed, waiting for him to crack a smile or offer a word of encouragement, but he remained stone-faced, as if he wished he were back at his restaurant, keeping an eye on the lazy cooks, instead of watching his amazing daughter dominate the Wildcats in front of the whole town on a lovely summer evening.

Maybe it's a Chinese thing, I thought. Maybe they don't like to show emotion in public. Or maybe—I had no idea, but it didn't keep me from speculating—he wished he had a son instead of a daughter (as far as I could tell, Lori was an only child). Like everybody else, I knew about the Chinese preference for boys over girls. One of my co-workers, a single woman in her late thirties, had recently traveled to Shanghai to adopt a baby girl abandoned by her parents. She said the orphanages were full of them.

But if Happy Chang didn't love his daughter, how come he came to every game? For that matter, why did he let her play at all? My best guess—based on my own experience as a father—was that he simply didn't know what to make of her. In China, girls didn't play baseball. So what did it mean that Lori played the game as well or better than any American boy? Maybe he was divided in his own mind between admiring her talent and seeing it as kind of a curse, a symbol of everything that separated him from his own past. Maybe that was why he faithfully attended her games, but always sat scowling on the wrong side of the field, as if he were rooting for her opponents. Maybe his daughter was as unfathomable to him as my own son had been to me.

Like most men, I'd wanted a son who reminded me of myself as a kid, a boy who lived for sports, collected baseball cards, and hung pennants on his bedroom walls. I wanted a son who played tackle football down at the schoolyard with the other neighborhood kids and came home with ripped pants and skinned knees. I wanted a son I could take to the ballpark and play catch with in the backyard.

But Jason was an artistic, dreamy kid with long eyelashes and delicate features. He loved music and drew elaborate pictures of castles and clouds and fairy princesses. He enjoyed playing with his sisters' dolls and exhibited what I thought was an unhealthy interest in my wife's jewelry and high heels. When he was seven years old, he insisted on going out trick-or-treating dressed as Pocahontas. Everywhere he went, people kept telling him how beautiful he was, and it was impossible not to see how happy this made him.

Jeanie did her best to convince me that it wasn't a problem; she cut out magazine articles that said he was simply engaged in harmless "gender play," and recommended that we let him follow his heart and find his own way in the world. She scolded me for using words like sissy and wimp, and for trying to enforce supposedly outdated standards of masculinity. I tried to get with the program, but it was hard. I was embarrassed to be seen in public with my own son, as if he somehow made me less of a man.

It didn't help that Carl had three normal boys living right next door. They were always in the backyard kicking a soccer ball, tossing a football, or beating the crap out of one another. Sometimes they included my son in their games, but it wasn't much fun for any of them.

Jason didn't want to play Little League, but I made him. I thought putting on a uniform might transform him into the kind of kid I would recognize as my own. Despite the evidence in front of my face, I refused to believe you could be an American boy and not love baseball, and not want to impress your father with your athletic prowess.

It's easy to say you should just let a kid follow his heart. But what if his heart takes him places you don't want to go? What if your ten-year-old son wants to take tap-dancing lessons in a class full of girls? What if he's good at it? What if he tells you when he's fourteen that he's made it onto the chorus of *Guys and Dolls*, and expects you to be happy about this? What if when he's fifteen he tells you he's joined the Gay and Lesbian Alliance at his progressive suburban high school? What if this same progressive school has a separate prom for boys who want to go with boys, and girls who want to go with girls? Are you supposed to say, *Okay, fine, follow your heart, go to the prom with Gerald, just don't stay out too late*?

I only hit him that once. He said something that shocked me and I slapped him across the face. He was the one who threw the first punch, a feeble right cross that landed on the side of my head. Later, when I had time to think about it, I was proud of him for fighting back. But at the time, it just made me crazy. I couldn't believe the little faggot had hit me. The punch I threw in return is the one thing in my life I'll regret forever. I broke his nose, and Jeanie called the cops. I was taken from my house in handcuffs, the cries of my wife and children echoing in my ears. As I ducked into the patrol car, I looked up and saw Carl watching me from his front stoop, shaking his head and trying to comfort Marie, who for some reason was sobbing audibly in the darkness, like it was her own child whose face I'd bloodied in a moment of thoughtless rage.

Lori Chang kept her perfect game going all the way into the top of the fifth, when Pete Gonzalez, the Wildcats' all-star shortstop, ripped a two-out single to center. A raucous cheer erupted from the third-base dugout and bleachers, both of which had lapsed into a funereal silence over the past couple of innings. It was an electrifying sound, a collective whoop of relief, celebration, and resurgent hope.

On a psychological level, that one hit changed everything. It was as if the whole ballpark suddenly woke up to two very important facts: 1. Lori Chang was not, in fact, invincible, and 2. The Wildcats could actually still win. The score was only 1-0 in favor of the Ravens, a margin that had seemed insurmountable a moment ago but that suddenly looked a whole lot slimmer now that the tying run was standing on first with a lopsided grin on his face, shifting his weight from leg to leg like he needed to go to the bathroom.

The only person who didn't seem to notice that the calculus of the game had changed was Lori Chang herself. She stood on the mound with her usual poker face, an expression that suggested profound boredom more than it did killer concentration, and waited for Trevor Mancini to make the sign of the cross and knock imaginary mud off his cleats. Once he got himself settled, she nodded to the catcher and began her windup, bringing her arms overhead and lowering them with the painstaking deliberation of a Tai Chi master. Then she kicked high and whipped a fastball right at Trevor, a guided missile that thudded into his leg with a muffled whump, the sound of a broomstick smacking a rug.

"Aaah shit!" Trevor flipped his bat in the air and began hopping around on one foot, rubbing frantically at his leg. "Shit! Shit! Shit!"

I stepped out from behind the catcher and asked if he was okay. Trevor gritted his teeth and performed what appeared to be an involuntary bow. When he straightened up, he looked more embarrassed than hurt.

"Stings," he explained.

I told him to take his base and he hobbled off, still massaging the sore spot. A chorus of boos had risen from the third-base side, and I wasn't surprised to see that Carl was already out of the dugout, walking toward me with what could only be described as an amused expression.

"Well?" he said. "What're you gonna do about it?"

"The batter was hit by a pitch. It's part of the game."

"Are you kidding me? She threw right at him."

Right on schedule, Tim came trotting over to join us, followed immediately by Ray Santelli, who approached us with his distinctive pot-bellied swagger, radiating an odd confidence that made you forget that he was just a middle-aged chauffeur with a combover.

"What's up?" he inquired. "Somebody got a problem?"

"Yeah, me," Carl told him. "I got a problem with your sweet little pitcher throwing beanballs at my players."

"That was no beanball," I pointed out. "It hit him in the leg."

"So that's okay?" Carl was one of those guys who smiled when he was pissed off. "It's okay to hit my players in the leg?"

"She didn't do it on purpose," Santelli assured him. "Lori wouldn't do that."

"I don't know," Tim piped in. "It looked pretty deliberate from where I was standing."

"How would you know?" Santelli demanded, an uncharacteristic edge creeping into his voice. "Are you some kind of mind reader?"

"I'm just telling you what it looked like," Tim replied.

"Big deal," said Santelli. "That's just your subjective opinion."

"I'm an umpire," Tim reminded him. "My subjective opinion is all I have."

"Really?" Santelli scratched his head, feigning confusion. "I thought you guys were supposed to be objective. When did they change the job description?"

"All right," said Tim. "Whatever. It's my objective opinion, okay?"

"Look," I said. "We're doing the best we can."

"I sure as hell hope not," Carl shot back. "Or else we're in big trouble."

Sensing an opportunity, Santelli cupped his hands around his mouth and called out, "Hey Lori, did you hit that kid on purpose?"

Lori seemed shocked by the question. Her mouth dropped open and she shook her head back and forth, as if nothing could have been further from the truth.

"It slipped," she said. "I'm really sorry."

"See?" Santelli turned back to Tim with an air of vindication. "It was an accident."

"Jack?" Carl's expression was a mixture of astonishment and disgust. "You really gonna let this slide?"

I glanced at Tim for moral support, but his face was blank, pointedly devoid of sympathy. I wished I could have thought of something more decisive to do than shrug.

"What do you want from me?" There was a pleading note in my voice that was unbecoming in an umpire. "She said it slipped."

"Now wait a minute—" Tim began, but Carl didn't let him finish.

"Fine," he said. "The hell with it. If that's the way it's gonna be, that's the way it's gonna be. Let's play ball."

Carl stormed off, leaving the three of us standing by the plate, staring at his back as he descended into the dugout.

"You can't know what's in another person's heart." Santelli shook his head, as if saddened by this observation. "You just can't."

"Why don't you shut up," Tim told him.

Lori quickly regained her composure when play resumed. With runners on first and second, she calmly and methodically struck out Antoine Frye to retire the side. On her way to the dugout she stopped and apologized to Trevor Mancini, resting her hand tenderly on his shoulder. It was a classy move. Trevor blushed and told her to forget about it.

Ricky DiSalvo was on the mound for the Wildcats, and though he had nowhere near Lori's talent, he was pitching a solid and effective game. A sidearmer plagued by control problems and a lack of emotional maturity—I had once seen him burst into tears after walking five straight batters—Ricky had wisely decided that night to make his opponents hit the ball. All game long, he'd dropped one fat pitch after another right over the meatiest part of the plate.

The Ravens, a mediocre hitting team on the best of days, had eked out a lucky run in the second on a single, a stolen base, an overthrow, and an easy fly ball to right field that had popped out of Mark Diedrich's glove, but they'd been shut out ever since. Ricky's confidence had grown with each successive inning, and he was throwing harder and more skillfully than he had all game by the time Lori Chang stepped up to the plate with two outs in the bottom of the fifth.

I guess I should have seen what was coming. When I watched the game on cable access a week later, it all seemed painfully clear in retrospect, almost inevitable. But at the time, I didn't sense any danger. We'd had some unpleasantness the previous inning, but it had passed when Lori apologized to Trevor. The game had moved forward, slipping past the trouble as easily as water flowing around a rock.

I did notice that Lori Chang looked a little nervous in the batter's box, but that was nothing unusual. As bold and powerful as she was on the mound, Lori was a surprisingly timid hitter. She tucked herself into an extreme crouch, shrinking the strike zone down to a few inches, and tried to wait out a walk. She rarely swung and was widely, and fairly, considered to be an easy out.

For some reason, though, Ricky seemed oddly tentative with his first couple of pitches. Ball one kicked up dirt about ten feet from the plate. Ball two was a mile outside.

"Come on," Carl called impatiently from the dugout. "Just do it."

Lori tapped the fat end of her bat on the plate. I checked my clicker and squatted into position. Ricky glanced at his father and started into his herky-jerky windup.

On TV, it all looks so fast and clean—Lori gets beaned and she goes down. But on the field it felt slow and jumbled, my brain lagging a beat behind the action. Before I can process the fact that the ball's rocketing toward her head, Lori's already said, "Ooof!" Her helmet's in the air before I register the sickening crack of impact, and by then she's already crumpled on the ground. On TV, it looks as though I move quickly, rolling her onto her back and coming in close to check her breathing, but in my memory it's as if I'm paralyzed, as if the world has stopped and all I can do is stare at the bareheaded girl lying motionless at my feet.

Then the quiet bursts into commotion. Tim's right beside me, shouting, "Is she okay? Is she okay?" Ricky's moving toward us from the mound, his glove pressed to his mouth, his eyes stricken with terror and remorse.

"Did I hurt her?" he asks. "I didn't mean to hurt her."

"I think you killed her," I tell him, because as far as I can tell, Lori's not breathing.

Ricky stumbles backwards, as if someone's pushed him. He turns in the direction of his father, who's just stepped out of the dugout.

"You shouldn't have made me do that!" Ricky yells.

"Oh my God," says Carl. He looks pale and panicky.

At that same moment, Happy Chang's scaling the third-base fence and sprinting across the infield to check on his daughter's condition. At least that's what I think he's doing, right up to the moment when he veers suddenly toward Carl, emitting a cry of guttural rage, and tackles him savagely to the ground.

Happy Chang is a small man, no bigger than some of our Little Leaguers, and Carl is tall and bulked up from years of religious weightlifting, but it's no contest. Within seconds, Happy's straddling Carl's chest and punching him repeatedly in the face, all the while shouting what must be very angry things in Chinese. Carl doesn't even try to defend himself, not even when Happy Chang reaches for his throat.

Luckily for Carl, two of our local policemen—Officers Freylinghausen and Hughes, oddly enough, the same two who'd arrested me for domestic battery—are present at the game, and before Happy Chang can finish throttling Carl, they've rushed the field and broken up the fight. They take Happy Chang into custody with a surprising amount of force—with me they were oddly polite—Freylinghausen grinding his face into the dirt while Hughes slaps on the cuffs. I'm so engrossed by the spectacle that I don't even realize that Lori's regained consciousness until I hear her voice.

"Daddy?" She says the word quietly, and for a second I think she's talking to me.

My whole life fell apart after I broke my son's nose. By the time I got out on bail the next morning, Jeanie had already taken the kids to her mother's house and slapped me with a restraining order. The day after that she started divorce proceedings.

In the year that had passed since then, nothing much had changed. I had tried apologizing in a thousand different ways, but it didn't seem to matter. As far as Jeanie was concerned, I'd crossed some unforgivable line, and was beyond redemption.

I accepted the loss of my wife as a fair punishment for what I'd done, but it was harder to accept the loss of my kids. I had some visiting rights, but they were severely restricted. Basically, I took my daughters—they were eleven and thirteen—to the movies or the mall every other Saturday, then to a restaurant, and then back to their grandmother's. They weren't allowed to stay overnight with me. It killed me to walk past their empty rooms at night, to not find them asleep and safe, and to be fairly sure I never would.

Once in a while Jason joined us on our Saturday excursions, but usually he was too busy with his plays. He had just finished his junior year in high school, capping it off with a starring role in the spring musical, *Joseph and the Amazing Technicolor Dreamcoat*. People kept telling me how great he was, and I kept agreeing, embarrassed to confess that I hadn't seen the show. My son had asked me not to come and I'd respected his wishes.

A year on my own had given me a lot of time to think, to come to terms with what had happened, and to accept my own responsibility for it. It also gave me a lot of time to stew in my own anger, to indulge the conviction that I was a victim too, every bit as much as my wife and son. I wrote Jeanie and my kids a lot of letters trying to outline my complicated position on these matters, but no one ever responded to them. It was like my side of the story had disappeared into some kind of void.

That's why I wanted so badly for my family to watch the championship game on cable access. I had e-mailed them all separately, telling them when it would be broadcast, and asking them to please tune in. I called them the day it aired, and left a message reminding them to be sure to stick it out all the way to the end.

What I wanted them to see was the top of the sixth and final inning, the amazing sequence of events that took place immediately following the beanball fiasco, after both Carl and Ricky DiSalvo had been ejected from the game, and Happy Chang had been hauled off to the police station.

Despite the fact that she'd been knocked unconscious just a few minutes earlier, Lori was back on the mound for the Ravens. She'd been examined and given a clean bill of health by Sharon Nelson, whose son, Daniel, played second base for the Wildcats. Dr. Nelson assured us that Lori hadn't suffered a concussion, and was free to continue playing if she felt up to it.

She started out strong, striking out Jeb Partridge and retiring Hiro Tamanaki on an easy infield fly. But then something happened. Maybe the blow to the head had affected her more seriously than she'd let on, or maybe she'd been traumatized by her father's arrest. Whatever the reason, she fell apart. With only one out remaining in the game, she walked three straight batters to load the bases.

I'd always admired Lori's regal detachment, her ability to remain calm and focused no matter what was going on, but now she just looked scared. She cast a desperate glance at the first base dugout, silently pleading with her coach to take her out of the game, but Santelli ignored her. No matter how badly she was pitching, she was still his ace. And besides, the next batter was Mark Diedrich, the Wildcats' pudgy right fielder, one of the weakest hitters in the league.

"Just settle down," Santelli told her. "Strike this guy out and we can all go home."

Lori nodded skeptically and got herself set on the mound. Mark Diedrich greeted me with a polite nod as he stepped into the batter's box. He was a nice kid, a former preschool classmate of my youngest daughter.

"I wish I was home in bed," he told me.

The first pitch was low. Then came a strike, the liveliest breaking ball Lori had thrown all inning, but it was followed by two outside fastballs (Ricky's beanball had clearly done the trick; Lori wasn't throwing anywhere near the inside corner). The next pitch, low and away, should have been ball four, but inexplicably, Mark lunged at it, barely nicking it foul.

"Oh Jesus," he whimpered. "Why did I do that?"

So there we were. Full count, bases loaded, two out. Championship game. A score of 1-0. The whole season narrowing down to a single pitch. If the circumstances had been a little different, it would have been a beautiful moment, an umpire's dream.

But for me, the game barely existed. All I could think of just then was the smile on Happy Chang's dirty face as the cops led him off the field. I was kneeling on the ground trying to comfort Lori, when Happy turned in our direction and said something low and gentle in Chinese, maybe asking if she was all right or telling her not to worry. Lori said something back, maybe that she was fine or that she loved him.

"Easy now," Santelli called from the dugout. "Right down the middle."

Lori tugged her shirt down in the back and squinted at the catcher. Mark Diedrich's face was beet red, as if something terribly embarrassing were about to happen.

"Please God," I heard him mutter as Lori began her windup. "Don't let me strike out."

I should have been watching the ball but instead I was thinking about Happy Chang and everything he must have been going through at the police station, the fingerprinting, the mug shot, the tiny holding cell. But mainly it was the look on his face that haunted me, the proud and defiant smile of a man at peace with what he'd done and willing to accept the consequences.

The ball smacked into the catcher's mitt, waking me from my reverie. Mark hadn't swung. As far as I could determine after the fact, the pitch appeared to have crossed the plate near the outside corner, though possibly a bit on the high side. I honestly didn't know if it was a ball or a strike.

I guess I could have lied. I could have called strike three and given the game to the Ravens, to Lori Chang and Ray Santelli. I could have sent Mark Diedrich sobbing back to the dugout, probably scarred for life. But instead I pulled off my mask.

"Jack?" Tim was standing between first and second with his palms open to the sky. "You gonna call it?"

"I can't," I told him. "I didn't see it."

There was a freedom in admitting it that I hadn't anticipated, and I dropped my mask to the ground. Then I slipped my arms through the straps of my chest protector and let that fall, too.

"What happened?" Mark Diedrich asked in a quavery voice. "Did I strike out?"

"I don't know," I told him.

Boos and angry cries rose from the bleachers as I made my way toward the pitcher's mound. I wanted to tell Lori Chang that I envied her father, but I had a feeling she wouldn't understand. She seemed relieved when I walked past her without saying a word. Mikey Fellner was out of the dugout and videotaping me as I walked past second base and onto the grass. He followed me all the way across centerfield, until I climbed the fence over the ad for the Prima Ballerina School of Dance and left the ballpark.

That's what I wanted my ex-wife and children to see—an umpire walking away from a baseball game, a man who had the courage to admit that he'd failed, who understood that there were times when you had no right to judge, responsibilities you were no longer qualified to exercise. I hoped they might learn something new about me, something I hadn't been able to make clear to them in my letters and phone calls.

But of course I was disappointed. What's in your heart sometimes remains hidden, even when you most desperately want it to be revealed. I remembered my long walk across the outfield as a dignified, silent journey, but on TV I seem almost to be jogging. I look sweaty and confused, a little out of breath as I mumble a string of barely audible excuses and apologies for my strange behavior. If Jeanie and the kids had been watching, all they would have seen was an unhappy man they already knew too well fleeing from the latest mess he'd made: just me, still trying to explain. ✧

# Salt Hill

Salt Hill is published by a group of writers affiliated with the Creative Writing Program at Syracuse University.

We welcome submissions of poetry, prose, translations, reviews, essays, interviews, and art work. We hold annual fiction and poetry contests (Postmark Deadline: January 15th). Send us an e-mail or visit our web site for submission guidelines and contest information.

*Recent contributors include Kim Addonizio, Steve Almond, Nin Andrews, Peter H. Conners, Brian Evenson, Maurice Guevara, Mark Halliday, Dan Pope, D. A. Powell, Amanda Stern, Terese Svoboda, James Tate, and Dean Young.*

Subscriptions:
*$15/year (individuals). $20/year (institutions)*
Sample copies available for $8 ($11 foreign)

Salt Hill
Syracuse University
English Department
Syracuse NY 13244
salthill@cas.syr.edu
http://students.syr.edu/salthill

# NONFICTION

# Yellow Pajamas

Derek Lance Furr

The last time I saw my grandfather, about three weeks before cancer finished the remnants of his visceral organs, he was in pajamas—yellow pajamas, cotton, with marigold trim. My grandmother was there, too, in the shadows behind him. It was a Saturday, my grandparents' fifty-first wedding anniversary. Withered and gnarled, my grandfather was hunched over in his recliner, his hands drawn into the cuffs of his sleeves, his knees pulled tight against his chest. Jaundice had stained his sunken cheeks. The blue of his terrified eyes floated, absurd, in the color of daffodils.

I was flummoxed by this encounter for many reasons, but all of them were concentrated in the fact of my grandfather—the brooding and sometimes severe patriarch of our family, whom everyone called "Papa John"—in pajamas. I had spent much of my life under Papa John's roof, and had only seen him in two stages of dress: fully covered in Pointer brand overalls—the kind worn by railroad engineers in children's books—and stark naked. Coming in from the barn at the end of the day, he would strip down on the back porch, shower, and blaze through the living room, a vapor trail of Ivory soap and red clay following him. He was shameless in his strong, hairy body, which filled the recliner as he ate his bowl of mashed potatoes and watched *Gunsmoke*. That's where he'd often sleep, naked and full, until he woke the next morning and, pulling on his overalls, headed back to work.

When I was little, I had once asked Papa John why he never wore pajamas. He spat a stream of tobacco juice into the bucket by his chair, reached over and turned up Matt Dillon before he chuckled, "They get all twisted and bind me up." My grandfather was not a man to be shackled. He made his own way among the hills and swamps of our tiny, rural community in North Carolina. He pursued his interests, acted on his whims. He moonshined and fished with dynamite. He raised barns, dug wells, cleared acres of pine for a sawmill he built of spare parts and sheer determination. He could grow any plant in creation, and his acres of vegetable gardens—irrigated by a complex system of pipe, pumps and ponds that he'd devised—overfed the twenty of us in his clan. When he was angry, he destroyed things; when happy, he laughed himself into paroxysms of coughing. We regarded him with the fearful respect that sustains gods and kings.

So finding him in yellow pajamas, his eyes swollen with hapless tears, I wanted to turn away. It was as if I had walked in on something that

I shouldn't see, something forbidden. I thought of Lear, in his torn white gown, his countenance frozen in a look of disbelief, blubbering piteously over his daughter's lifeless body. For a moment, Lear doesn't know we're there, and should we be? What can you say or do when you see someone so reduced?

Illness and injury often humble us, shaming us into acknowledging our limitations. But Papa John had always scoffed at pain. He rarely went to the doctor and never took medicine. Most aches or ailments could be ignored altogether, he suggested, and even the most grievous conditions could be endured with true grit and, perhaps, a few shots of Wild Turkey. About a decade before I was born, Papa John's right arm was cut off by a silage cutter. "Chewed" would be the more appropriate verb, for as he tried to dislodge a knot of silage from the machine's throat, it sucked him in and ground to a halt at his elbow, not sated but choked again. In the trauma ward for days thereafter, my grandfather refused to be treated for pain. "You get dependent on those drugs," he declared, and no amount of suffering was going to steal his rugged independence. At least not until the end stages of cancer.

On that Saturday, I nodded to him and awkwardly slipped away to a corner of the room that was partially blocked from view by the wood stove. The rest of our family began to crowd in, all of them from just down the road and bearing dishes of various descriptions for the potluck. Because I had traveled several hundred miles to return home for the first time in months, my presence provided some distraction—welcomed, I imagined, as a momentary ballast to suffering and disillusionment.

For a while my aunts and mother chattered about my weight, or lack of it, and the circles under my eyes, about how I needed to eat more and stop staying up so late reading books and worrying. My wife Caroline had recently assumed the yoke of the good partner—mediating between spouse and family—and steered the conversation away from my health, offering up anecdotes about our drive down with our neurotic dachshund howling in the back seat. Most of us chuckled. Among the women, only my grandmother remained silent, vigilantly on call behind Papa John, the only man who hadn't at least smiled or blushed at Caroline's monologue. Then with sighs and winks, all the women save Grandma retreated to the kitchen, and the men of my family were left to their own, limited conversational devices.

My father and three uncles, each leaning back in a wooden chair dragged from the kitchen, stared awkwardly at their empty hands. My brother pretended to study a seed catalog that he had plucked from the otherwise empty magazine rack. Finally, Uncle Wes inquired, "How's the weather up north?" My home in Charlottesville, Virginia, is "the north" to my family, a peculiar land of harsh winters and impractical ambitions.

"We've had our share of it!" I declared, and my uncle nodded as if he understood. The silence resumed, denser now for having resisted our paltry attempt to fill it. The tocks of the clock on the mantle plopped into it like stones in a lake. Everyone stared holes in his hands. Tucked safely behind the stove, I stole glimpses at my grandfather.

It was now that Papa John had always saved us in the past. He'd get a story started. First he'd toss out an apparently artless observation about farming or hunting or mechanics. "The dry rot's going to eat up half the tomato crop this year." "Deer's been using the hollow. Got the bark rubbed clean off that big cedar." "Head gasket on the GMC needs replacing." Invariably, someone would rise to the bait, giving Papa John a moment to light a cigarette—Camels, filterless, their fine Turkish blend holding the mysteries of the Orient. He would inhale long and deep while, for example, my father described the buck he'd jumped when walking the fence line, and then he'd exhale two billowing streams of aromatic smoke from his nostrils. A haze would gather in the room, soporific, even a bit intoxicating, and Papa John would deftly pick up a thread from my father's disquisition and spin it into a yarn from his past.

Today, however, it was as if that past had been razed and burned by the cancer. Those shanty towns of fops and shrews who populated Papa John's irreverent version of our family history were smoke and ash. He had no stories to tell—intense suffering had pinned him to the present. He stared at the window shades, a flinch and an attenuated cough his only vital signs. Grandma lingered behind him, an apparition, like his broken spirit.

Simply sitting in the presence of pain takes discipline. I squirmed. The temptation to narrative in such circumstances is understandable. Was it up to me, I wondered, to get a story going? Narrative organizes, interprets, distracts. For those very reasons, however, it had no place here. Job's companions should have just kept their mouths shut. I settled into the darkness.

But then a cake was brought in. The piping, the butter cream roses, the cursive wishes for a "Happy Fifty First," all were yellow. And on a tiny porcelain plate in the center were two gold wedding bands. Caroline ran ahead of the cake like a scout. She crouched by my knees and squeezed my hand, as she does when the plane hits turbulence on its descent.

And that's as much of the day as I can remember. My memory's stage goes dark just as Caroline clutches my hand, and the cake, like the Ark of the Covenant in its uncanny symbolic heft, is borne in. In truth, some time in the years that intervened between that day and my recollection of it, I even lost the rings. The cake I still saw, but the rings—which promise to focus the sad plot of that anniversary gathering, to complicate it and drive it irrevocably forward—were gone. Instead, it was the ruins of my grandfather, tricked up so absurdly in the colors of spring, that filled the day's space in my memory. The wedding bands reappeared in the rubble only after Caroline, reading an earlier version of this essay, pointed them out to me.

My grandparents had been too poor to afford the extravagance of rings when they'd eloped on Papa John's furlough from the army. They'd been too practical to consider buying them later. Love, they believed, inheres in the sacrifices you make for the well-being of your family. Doing without carries more weight than gold.

My mother produced the anniversary gathering and insisted upon wedding bands. She was determined to lay claim to joy despite the omnipresence of sorrow, and she wanted in particular to do something to bolster Grandma. For under the influence of intractable misery during his dying days, Papa John had been relentlessly cruel to Grandma. Pain had whipped his demons into a fury. A man of his era, he unleashed them on his wife, who fussed at his sheets and pillows and freshened his watery Coca-Cola in a futile attempt to comfort him. Grandma had endured, but her daughter, understandably, agonized. "Mama must not feel unloved," my mother thought, "not now." Plans were made. A cake was baked and decorated. Rings were bought.

I don't recall the look on Grandma's face, or whether she and Papa John cut the cake. Did they feed it to each other? And the wedding bands—were they worn? Was one on Papa John's hand at his wake a few weeks later? There's a tale filled with irony and pathos in all this, a tale of well-intended gestures, hapless victims, maudlin sentiment. But it's not the tale I remember, or wish to reconstruct, though there are pictures and witnesses at my disposal. For me, the suffering of that day and that period in my family's life is summed up at the vanishing point in my own memory. And what I remember, finally, of that day, are Caroline's grasp—a warning, a reassurance, a commiseration—and how my grandfather's eyes, filled with pain, matched his pajamas and the roses on the cake and the burn of the sunlight through the drawn shades.  ✧

# Two Birds

Jim Dameron

**A** crow made me flinch. I ducked my head, hunched my shoulders, lost the easy grace of riding my bike and swerved a little. My heart raced, and for just a moment I was confused. In another second my muscles would push me to flee, but in that first instant I felt exposed, as if I had forgotten some primordial lesson.

Pedaling along I had been oblivious to everything except the sun and the cooling breeze. Then that crow sailed over my head, completely minding its own business. But its shadow loomed, and for a moment I forgot that crows don't eat bicycle riders.

No big deal. Still, I didn't like that involuntary cringe, that shrinking from an imagined pounce, that pre-conscious sense that it was already too late. No matter how absurd the scene I felt hunted, and I started to think about what it's like to be prey. But that crow nudged me toward cunning, not empathy, and my first reaction was to reassert my claim to the top of the food chain.

So, the next time I went trout fishing I began stalking those fish; I didn't want to be a clumsy crow needlessly frightening my quarry. With a little practice I've gotten good at it. In fact, my waders have a hole in the knee from crawling to the river. I look like a supplicant to the uninitiated, but I also fancy myself a hunter, though perhaps a fastidious one. I move sideways, stay low, never directly walk to the river bank. I creep up on things.

As a result, only a week ago I found myself crouched over, standing on one foot staring at a great blue heron. I had never been so close to the bird some people call the big crank. I could clearly see the white of its long lower bill and a tan spot in its wing. I could see azure and cobalt and black feathers. The heron balanced on one skinny leg, held its ground and stared back at me.

I stood on my right foot for as long as I could, but try as I might, I couldn't hold the position. I started to wobble and the stiff fabric of my waders cracked and creaked as my left leg rubbed my right. Thinking that the heron would jump into the sky with my next step, I inched forward and kept my eyes on that cranky bird. I imagined it leaping upward, hanging for a moment on elbowy wings. Feathers would rustle and strain with displaced air; overextended wing tips would stretch and flick against tree limbs and shrubs.

I settled onto two feet expecting an uproar, but the bird only turned a single eye to look at me more closely. I took another cautious step, then another. The bird grew indifferent, turned its head away, stayed put. I moved toward the water. The heron lingered. Then, in what seemed a complete lapse of character, it tucked its bony knees and yellow-gray legs and lanky body into a scruffy ball and flung itself into the river. After a noiseless splash it bounced up and down for an instant, then calmly eased itself back to the bank.

But what about hunting I wondered, what about that slow tiptoeing toward lunch? I felt tricked; worse, I felt mocked. The heron represented my prototypical hunter, yet here it was goofing off, horsing around. It didn't look malnourished, didn't appear as if in danger of missing its next meal, so why didn't it share my adherence to a knee-scraping regime?

Baffled, I stood up straight, wiped the dirt from my waders, took a step into the water and cast my fly line upstream. Usually when I fish, I have a delicate touch, a light hand. Perhaps it's only a conceit, but I believe my casts are pretty, slow, precise. I can put my fly where I want it. In such fashion I aspire to perfection—I must breathe just right, pull my line off the water with steady tugs, toss it over my shoulder into a tight back cast, start it forward only after it has completely unfurled. I want my fly to descend from the sky as if it had veined wings of its own.

Yet if the glinting sun hides the water's depth, if I forget the reminder that good anglers ask good questions, if I take too much pride in casting for its own sake, I can hypnotize myself. Over and over again I place the same fly upon the same piece of water. And what was delicate becomes mechanical. What began with the stealthy approach and a systematic search becomes a numb lingering in place. What was curiosity and observation is transformed into the worst sort of repeated ritual. As a result, the light touch is lost, the crow's shadow forgotten, and I leave with an aching shoulder.

So, of course I wasn't catching any fish, even though I could occasionally see rainbow trout roiling just below the surface, even though I saw steelhead, red and green and shimmery, arch in and out of the water as if they might baste river to sky. Even though I heard a guy fishing just downstream yell to his buddy, "Salmon! A big one."

By this time I was deep into the river, but I reeled in my line, struggled back to shore and sat down next to a spiky hackberry tree. I would watch for a while. The two anglers, noting my absence, slowly converged on the stretch of river I had just vacated. And they did exactly what I feared they would do. They caught fish even though their casts were rough and their lines whipped the water. Back and forth they continued to yell at each other—*try a number sixteen green worm, a brown soft hackle, a hare's ear.*

I suppose I could argue that my desire to catch fish has weakened, that I have a half-formed urge to leave the creatures be. I might hypothesize that I've spent too much time in the company of river biologists, switched allegiances, lost the blood rush of the serious hunter. For symmetry's sake, I could add that I've come to love the river itself—its pulse, its changes—and want desperately to catch it in the act. But here's another truth: that heron and those shouting anglers stick in my craw.

The surprise of a flashing trout still excites. The logic of hooked fish as answered riddle still satisfies.

I understand that trout aren't puzzles and herons don't dawdle on river banks to give out free advice. But I wanted to grab hold of that heron's meaning, to collapse the gulf between us. When I swayed on one foot in its presence I stood before a huge, ferocious bird—herons are four feet tall and have six foot wing spans. A friend once watched a blue heron kill a green heron that had poached on its territory—the blue heron just reached over and speared it dead.

And yet I cannot fully explain the appeal of this bird by only citing its size and its ferocity; I've had similar feelings in the presence of ruby-crowned kinglets and brown creepers. Face to face, these hollow-boned, light-as-a-feather birds appear dense, impenetrable. And irreducibly beautiful. I can't explain it away: after I account for iridescence as an optical property of feathers, after I take stock of the curved wing that produces lift and the bird melody that precedes copulation, beauty remains. Nor can I shake it off with a subjective flick of my hand: this beauty isn't a construct, a learned pattern, an interpretation of sensory data taking place within my skull. No, the heron's beauty has its own logic, its own luminescence; it doesn't require an opposite, it stands apart from my need to name it.

What had started as a casual encounter with a stray bird seemed to grow in importance. I felt as if the answer to some half uttered secret lay within my reach. I wanted to anticipate the heron's movements, to render it predictable, to put a hammerlock on it. Yes, I wanted to know that bird. I felt the insistence of its contours, got an inkling of its edges, imagined its intent. I considered packing myself into a tight ball and jumping into the river. However ridiculous, I wanted to whisper to the heron, to surprise it, to wait patiently for it to whisper back.

But the anglers I scorned were closer to getting it right than I was. They, at least, had an ability to mess around, make a little noise, a big splash, engage in some fanciful misdirection. Their banter reminded me of two kids at play, and such playfulness suggests an open mind, a desire to consider multiple options, a willingness to hand over control, an ability to link ideas together. I, in contrast, am like a slow but unstoppable pendulum, sweeping from pole to pole, seeking dominance on the one side and a radical communion on the other. I haven't quite accepted the idea that awe and mystery do not represent a problem in need of a solution.

As I watched the river swirl past me, as I sifted the possibilities, that great heron took off in a ragged upward spiral. Just as it started to fold its neck into the posture of sustained flight, it fooled me again, and instead of continuing straight down the river, it veered to its left and landed high in a ponderosa pine. And there it sat, seemingly too large, too angular for such a narrow perch. But the bird with the telescopic sight turned a yellow eye toward the river below and settled in. I could only wonder at what it would do next.  ✧

# Hitting Harmony

Nathan Ihara

I am now twenty-three and all I can think about is how that's the same age Harmony Korine was when I wrote E-N-V-Y on my fist and socked him in the head. I was eighteen when I did it, and more obsessed with Harmony than I've been with any director, rapper, writer, rock-star, anyone.

When I read that Harmony was having an art opening at the Patrick Painter Gallery in Santa Monica, I called my friend Nick Lowe and said, "Nick, man, Harmony's coming to town. We *have* to beat him up!" I felt queasy and eager, as if someone had dared me to kiss a girl or jump naked into a lake.

Nick started cracking up when he heard my plan; he loved the idea. I knew Nick would understand. In high school Nick had gone to see John Waters—one of *his* early artistic influences—sign books, and since Nick didn't have a book he asked Waters to sign his penis instead (Waters cheerfully obliged).

But a few days later Nick backed out of the plan. "While I fully support *you* punching Harmony Korine," he said, "I don't think *I* should play a part in the fight. This is *your* project." I gave him a hard time about it, but finally I forgave him. I couldn't stay angry with someone who called my loopy impulse a "project."

My roommate Madeline also empathized. Little Madeline, petite, dressed like a French school boy out of "The 400 Blows," asexual and serious (her lesbian relationships were still a few years down the road)—she looked at me and asked, "Are you really going to do that? Are you serious?" She wasn't accusing or doubting me. In fact, her voice was slightly awestruck, as if my idea was the smartest thing she had ever heard.

Madeline was an intern on the 20th Century Fox studio lot, and she spent her lunch breaks stalking Gillian Anderson (Special Agent Dana Scully), or rather, lingering unnecessarily outside the *X-Files* sound stage. For an art project (we were both art majors at the University of California, Los Angeles, had both recently failed to get into the film school) she shot hundreds of Polaroids of Scully's freeze-framed face and displayed them on a fluorescent light-table, as if they were evidence from some autopsy. She said that she wanted to "show how our consumption of trivial facets and details of mass culture has taken on an almost scientific morbidity—" blah blah blah. I thought all her talk was just a cerebral windshield for Madeline's more desperate cravings.

It's the same for me with Harmony. I'd like to put some intellectual spin on what I did, but the emotions are, finally, embarrassingly simple. At the heart of the matter is *Gummo*, Harmony's first film.

*

The movie opens and closes with tornado footage, and the tornado (with its fusion of chaos and eerie order) is the driving metaphor of the film. Set in Xenia, Ohio, *Gummo* depicts a desperate, stupid, vile and anarchistic white-trash wonderland. The film abandons linearity, skipping helter-skelter from found-footage to documentary, from blotchy video images to grainy stills. Beer-swilling rednecks wrestle a chair. A black dwarf rejects the sexual advances of a weepy drunk (played by Harmony). Two grown identical twins wash each other in a small bathtub. In a pool in the rain, two sisters take turns catching and kissing a waifish boy wearing a pink bunny hat.

And then the storm finally arrives. The "Bunny-Boy" runs through the downpour and holds one last murdered cat accusatorily toward the screen and the audience. Then the tornadoes come. The sky goes dark with flying leaves. Roy Orbison's "Crying" wails in the background. The sun shimmers behind the writhing twisters. Houses and windows crack, the camera shakes, and the air takes horrible shape.

The first time I saw the film, in the final tornado montage, I started screaming at the screen. I smacked the back of the seat in front of me with my hands. I felt great, dizzy, like I was rich, like my name had been pulled out of a hat. I hissed, whistled, I laughed my stupid head off. But the dozens of times I've watched the film since, the final tornado footage makes me want to despair. I can't think of a single other movie that I've cried at, but, as Orbison warbles and the tornadoes turn the world upside down, something in my chest seizes up, and I lose it.

*Gummo* became my personal model for a "great" film, one that performs a balancing act between fantasy and documentary. Harmony rejects the (still) popular notion of the director as a grand tyrant stamping his artistic OK on every aspect of a film. Instead of a director, I think of Harmony as a lion-tamer—the drama of his "act" is the tension between his personal aesthetic and the capricious nature of his subjects.

One summer I worked at a small video store in New York City. One of the other employees, Mitch, had worked as a production assistant on *Gummo*, one of the few professionally trained members of the film crew. He thought Harmony was a joke. "The guy didn't do anything! The cinematographer [Jean-Yves Escoffier] did all the real work, and the actors had to come up with all the scenes and lines on their own. He just ran around like a stupid fucking kid saying, 'That's cool! Yeah! Do more of that!'"

What Mitch wanted, obviously, was a "real" director, someone to control the film. Harmony has no interest in this. In an interview with artist Mike Kelly, Harmony said, "We tried really hard to have images come from all directions. If I had to give this style a name, I'd call it a 'mistake-ist' art form—like science projects, things blowing up in my face."

For example, in *Gummo* a child in pink bunny ears, short-shorts, and plastic flip-flops walks into a junkyard, and is attacked by two scrawny kids, brothers, dressed up as cowboys, and weilding cap-guns. "I hate fucking rabbits!" One of the kids shouts at the Bunny-Boy. The oldest is seven or eight years old, tops, the other a few years younger. "Goddamn rabbit!" The boys fire their puny pistols and the Bunny-Boy falls to the mud, dead. They stand over him, howling and cussing, "Rabbits come into my fucking house I kill 'em! Look at his fag bunny ears! He smells like pussy! He smells like an asshole! He smells like a big dick. HE SMELLS LIKE A PILE OF BULLSHIT!"

The Bunny-Boy is a kind of white-trash totem animal. He wanders, mute and magical, through Harmony's Xenia. In a doorless bathroom stall, the Bunny-Boy plays the film's droning accordian theme song. He is a creature of fantasy (born, no doubt, from *Freaks*, *Los Olvidados*, *La Strada*), a shard of Harmony's imagination.

The cowboy brothers, however, are pure documentary. Even if their roles seem familiar, there's something about their lispy hate, the unadulterated spit and ignorance of their words that exists outside the artificiality of film-making. Like the lion tamer's lions, they are alive. Perhaps they have been led, duped even, onto Harmony's vaudevillian stage and forced to interact with the whimsical Bunny-Boy, but for a brief moment they are so dangerous and present that there is no denying them.

What are we to make of this scene? Do we classify it as an imaginative construction or as an unsettling moment of documentary? Both, of course, and neither. It is the "Reality TV" principle taken to the millionth power. It's Chris Burden crucified on a Volkswagen bug. It's Andy Kaufman riling thousands of Memphian wrestling fans. The Bunny-Boy is fake, a piece of fancy. The children are real, ferociously so. Art and reality meet in the junkyard (it could have been a country club, a suburban dining room, it doesn't matter), equally matched, and grapple there.

Another reason *Gummo* hit me so hard is because it all seemed so damn familiar. The film could easily have been set in my hometown, Manila, California, Pop. 1000, Elev. 0, a cluster of houses and trailers strewn along a sandy peninsula on the northwest coast of the state.

I remember walking down the railroad tracks near my house and being accosted by two freckled blonde brothers (in my memory their faces have actually been replaced by the *Gummo* kids). "You fucking hippie faggot!" one shouted. "Hippie faggot!" the younger one chimed in.

I was a senior in high school, in jeans and a T-shirt, and with only the slightest suggestion of a George Harrison haircut (circa '66). "What exactly makes me a hippie or a faggot?" I asked the older brother. He sucked in his breath, and in one bilious exhalation, screamed, "Because your face looks like my ass crack! AND YOU SMELL LIKE SHIT!" As I walked away, the younger brother hurled a pebble at my back.

I know those are his exact words because I wrote them down as soon as I got home and used them later in a short story. Unlike most of the kids in Manila, I wasn't poor, but the "white-trash lifestyle" was all around me. A family died when the father's meth-cooking operation blew them to pieces. Our neighbor Ralph choked to death on his own vomit, his wife, Lily, unconscious beside him. The town's only gas station shut down before I was born, the pump nozzles splayed, the gallon and dollar dials rusted to oo.oo. Local kids knocked the City Limits sign off its post and threw it in a ditch. When I tried to stop Brady O'Leary, age ten, from thrashing his dog with a chain, he whined at me, "Why not? Jesus, it is my dog." When my sister borrowed some sugar for cookies one Christmas, there was a warning note in the jar: *Careful! Sugar.*

In high school most of my stories and Super 8 films were about Manila. Though not exactly part of it, I was intoxicated by the grain and texture of these lives. Everything seemed rawer, more immediate, for these people, especially the children. Despite the meanness and bigotry, there was something perversely enchanting to me about their knee-jerk existences. It was the whole "Noble Savage" idea, minus the nobleness.

One of my short stories from that time describes Manila's mythological origins: the town was born as trash washed up by the ocean. Wire, chain-link, fiberglass, tires, and broken glass discarded by other, nicer, coastal towns accumulated on a shoal. The detritus slowly formed structure: shacks, old cars, sheds, trailers, railroad tracks. People suddenly appear, scuttling like homeless hermit crabs out of the drift-junk, clutching salty clothes to their clammy bodies. Manila "thrives" for a short time. Kids scream, dogs howl, cats fuck. Then a huge wave rises out of the ocean; it sweeps over the peninsula, and, in a few clattering crashing minutes, takes back everything it has given.

This scenario is not, in fact, so far-fetched. Seismologists have predicted that the long dormant Cascadia fault line just off the coast of Manila could slip sometime in the next 50 years causing an 8.0 or higher on the Richter scale "megathrust" earthquake. The quake will launch a tsunami, a wavelength rippling through the ocean at 600 mph, invisible until it reaches the shallows.

Then, suddenly, the tide will rise eighty feet, battering the town with debris-choked water. Next the tide will drop eighty feet, exposing sea-weed and gasping fish. This trough and wave combination will pummel the town seven to twelve times in only an hour. Like a sand-castle in a rising tide, the entire peninsula could liquefy and crumble.

The last time the Cascadia fault shook—according to massive dis-turbance in the geologic record, Native American folktales, and Chinese historical records—was on January 26, 1700 A.D. Another is due. It could come any day. Growing up, this natural disaster both worried and delighted me; it was awful, but it also seemed to make sense.

What's significant here (as far as me punching Harmony is concerned) is that I was fumbling, in my mind and fiction, with nearly identical social setting and characters, and that I viewed these lives through the same calamity-tinted glasses. When I started shooting videos and super8 films (melodramatic pans of a busted Buick, "Eat Shit" graffitied on it), I was groping for something that I didn't understand yet. There was something there, and I wanted it. I just didn't know what "it" was. Or, I didn't know what "it" was until I saw *Gummo* and started screaming at the screen. And now we're starting to get to the heart of it. Because, the truth is, I never got a hold, never got my fingers around it. My "white-trash" films were sentimental hokum. They stank. They smelled like shit.

When I was thirteen, just beginning to jot down my sloppy adolescent thoughts, Harmony was in New York City selling his teen-ploitation screenplay *KIDS* to photographer Larry Clark. While Harmony was filming *Gummo*, I was shooting a video about dorm life (of all lame subjects). The year Harmony had his art opening, my biggest "achievement" was boxing with Nick in an alley and having some midnight "massage parlor" girls come out and watch.

Tomorrow it's the ripe old age of twenty-three, and artistically I don't have much to show for myself. My Manila movies are crappy, and I don't plan on making more. When I think about *Gummo* I feel robbed. An artist's childhood is his birthright, the stuff of his dreams and nightmares. Sure, there's always an endless supply of material to fuel painting, poetry, performance-fucking-art, but sometimes there's the one "big" work waiting to be made, the one "right" way to make it.

It can be humiliating to realize how simple one's psychology really is, how patently obvious the influences are. For years I thought punching Harmony was this mysterious chapter in my life, but looking back on it . . . Let's just say: I wrote E-N-V-Y on the fingers of one fist, and L-O-V-E on the fingers of the other. And then I went looking for trouble.

So I'm at the opening. It's at Patrick Painter Gallery at Bergamot Station, a handful of galleries and artist studios clumped around an asphalt courtyard. Though a few friends were also coming, I took the bus here alone. It was, I'd decided, my thing. Also I was sloshed. I had been drinking tequila all afternoon, and had a flask of Jose Cuervo in the back pocket of my jeans for nerves. I wore a white-trash outfit: my faded "work" jeans, the ones to get dirty in, and a car-mechanic shirt buttoned over a wife-beater. I wanted to be the kind of person Harmony would be interested in. I wanted to seem desperate and dumb, and I suppose, looking back on it, I was.

I arrived early, and Harmony was still putting the show up, making sure the artwork was properly hung, figuring out the labels and prices.

He seemed annoyed and nervous, like a kid before a recital or school play. He kept calling people on his cell phone; he sounded bratty.

Most of the details of the day are pretty foggy because of the tequila. I know the first time I talked to him he was sitting on the wine table watching the art-scene people arrive. I thought that the typical art gallery atmosphere of defensiveness (everyone worrying that their bluff will be called) was mixed with a dangerous buzz. Were there more freaks and riff-raff here than at most openings? Didn't everyone seem a little angry and crazed? It felt like everyone had something to prove.

*Gummo* is just great. Sure, he said. I told him that it did, captured, something I hadn't seen before. He shrugged that off. I told him that I fucked his grandmother (he lived with his grandmother for years), but couldn't keep a straight face while I said it. He wasn't impressed. I wanted to fight. He said that he didn't really feel like it. He excused himself, and joined a group of his friends who had arrived: a white guy with an afro, another in camouflage and big yellow sunglasses, etc. Harmony wore a white T-shirt and his beard was grown out all over his face, like some adolescent Mennonite. His skin was pasty and wet; he looked sick. I probably talked to him three or four more times that afternoon. He was mostly polite, somewhat annoyed. The way I imagine him, he always has a trace of sneer.

Finally I did it. People were mingling in front of the gallery, drinking, chatting. Harmony walked past and I ran two steps and punched him in the side of the head, just above the ear. Or maybe just below, near the joint of his jaw. I don't remember how hard it was, but I know it was loud. The feel of my knuckles on his head (the only physical contact we ever made) vanished in a rush of fear and adrenaline, but I can still hear the hollow clunking sound. Nick Lowe confirmed this with me later. "It was loud," he said, "everyone heard it."

What happened next seems hazy and dreamlike, especially the visuals (my glasses got knocked off at some point). Harmony didn't fall down, but moved (staggered?) away from me. Then he swung at me with something, but the people around us were already holding us back. So he started swearing, a rush of profanity: cocksucker, motherfucker, son of a mother fucking bitch!

He was snarling, hysterical. I'd only had children fling this kind of language at me before, and I was surprised to learn that it stung. It sounds slightly idiotic, considering the circumstances, but it hurt my feelings. I bounced back with some of my own ("Come on motherfucker, let's go!") but it sounded forced and theatrical. What was I talking about? What was I doing?

He screamed at me, "You son of bitch! You sucker punched me! I'll fucking kill you, man, I'm going to fucking kill you!" and, for the first time, it crossed my mind that punching someone might make them mad.

Up until then I had only been thinking of myself, of the moments leading up to this moment. And fighting Nick in the alley had always been intimate; afterwards, sweaty and hurting, Nick and I squatted on the concrete, leaned into each other, almost embraced. It was something we were doing together, a shared purpose. Harmony wasn't interested in sharing—he was pissed.

Some single-minded part of my brain had convinced me that this was something that *I had to do*, but now the voice in my head was sarcastic: Well that's just great, Nathan, *now you've done it!*

Nick had to fill me in on some of the best details later. First, I didn't realize what Harmony had tried to attack me with. "A crutch!" Nick told me, gleeful. "That lunatic pulled this lady's crutch out from under her." Harmony had immediately grasped the low drama of the situation and made it more raucous and exciting.

Another thing I had to be told later: several people started shooting the scene on their digital cameras, and when everything was over, there was scattered applause. The crowd thought the whole thing was planned. They thought it was art. *Harmony Korine's opening? Of course there will be a fight arranged.* But you do not arrange a besotted fan. These things happen by mistake.

After a minute or two, a security guard came and tossed me off the property. He was a black man, thin, past fifty, one of those security guards you see sometimes at banks or museums in their ironed pants and starched shirts, and can't help but wonder, "If push came to shove, what, exactly, would this poor old dude do?"

Well, what he did was wrap his arms under my armpits and across my chest and drag me backwards across the courtyard. There was something almost gentle about the way he held me. "Let go of me, man," I pleaded with him. "Please, come on, don't throw me out."

"You're bothering people here, son," I remember him saying softly in my ear. "I don't want anything bad to happen to you."

Between my wretched vision (no glasses), the adrenaline, and the tequila, the city was too loud and too bright. I walked around, found a nice telephone pole to lean against, and started bawling. I don't tell this part of the story most of the time, but the truth is, I felt miserable and stupid and lost. I was actually lucky: a few minutes after I was thrown out (I'm told) Harmony gathered up his buddies and went looking for me, presumably to do some real damage. I don't know how they missed me—I was only a few blocks away—but they did. Finally, I called a friend collect and asked him to pick me up.

Later, when Nick told me that he thought the "whole thing had gone really well," I felt a strange pride, as if I had done a good deed. When I heard that the fight was a topic of conversation at one party in East Hollywood, another in Silver Lake, I actually had the gall to say, "Yeah, I did that asshole a favor. Come on! This will help his reputation. You don't get to be an *enfant terrible* without taking your licks."

When Madeline came back to our apartment from school (she couldn't make it to the opening) she wanted to know the whole story. By then I'd been looking in the mirror, chatting on the phone, puffing myself up. Madeline sat on my futon, and I paced back and forth, the adrenaline running again, telling the story, adding the good parts about the crutch, the video cameras, the clapping. She was clearly impressed, even jealous. The closest she would ever get to Gillian Anderson was later that month when they bumped into each other coming around the corner of a building ("Just like something in a cartoon!" she would tell me).

"So why did you do it?" Madeline asked.

I'd been anticipating this question, and had come up with a first-class answer.

"I guess that's like asking Rauschenberg why he erased the de Kooning," I said. "Sometimes you can't just learn from the artists you admire or who came before you. Sometimes you have to delete them. You've got to make some grandiose gesture to get them off your back. The anxiety of influence and all that. You have to prove to yourself that they're nothing special, nothing sacred."

"Wow. I like that," she said. "Does that work?"

"Sure. Of course," I said. "Of course it does. Of course . . . "

Last year I moved out of Los Angeles to get a Masters in English in a college town in southern Mississippi. It is, of course, the poorest state, and I've heard a few good stories about the ways lives are lived, but that stuff doesn't seem as juicy anymore. I pretty much stick to the Liberal Arts Building and the Library. For Thanksgiving I went home to Manila, but I stayed inside my parents' house the whole weekend.

My television is on my bedside table and I watched *Gummo* twice yesterday, once in the morning, another time before falling asleep. I skimmed through parts, jumped around. It's flawed, I tell myself, it has all kinds of silly scenes, weak spots. I didn't cry at the end, wouldn't let myself. My own video camera is in the closet with the towels. The eye-piece is broken. I haven't pointed a film camera in years. I guess I've given it up.

I'm turning twenty-three tomorrow, and sometimes I wish I had another shot at Harmony. This time I'd fucking kill him.  ✧

# Blue Window

Liesl Schwabe

The room itself was nothing spectacular. The concrete floor, cold and slippery, made even the taboo of wearing shoes indoors a necessity in January. There was a basic attached bathroom; a squatty toilet, a sink, a round flat shower head that turned the whole room into the shower, an electrical hot water heater with "Geyser" printed in English in large silver letters, with a temperamental switch I would only fiddle with when wearing plastic slippers to ground me, and a window. The window opened and closed like a book, with the spine on the left. The wooden shutter and frame were painted a very particular shade of Indian blue, which I have tried to come up with a name for but for which I have no name. This blue does not occur in nature. As far as I know, no flower or fish or mold is quite this blue. It is a synthetic blue. It is a beautiful blue. It is bright and deliberate and everywhere in India. The shutter was equipped with a hook-and-eye latch that fit perfectly together. A latch where the hook does not quite reach the eye, or where it overextends, or for which it takes a fussy sort of pushing or pounding, is very frustrating. But a hook with an eye that slides in with just enough tension and precision is reassuring, some small proof of things being how they should.

The window itself was small and nearly square. There was no screen and no glass, only the blue wood shutter to distinguish inside from outside. Glass panes can make the outside seem so far away, flat and two-dimensional, like a painting. Being on the inside of glass, the outside seems almost optional, as if temperature or wind is a choice you have to consider. Without even a screen, the window becomes precisely that, a piece of the outside, inside; with all its properties of transition and inescapability; the warmth of spring air, the smell of dust, the sound of sickle on rice.

Out of the open blue window, all that could be seen were the explosive tops of the palm trees that grew from three stories down, at the edge of the rice paddy below. Every morning that I opened that window, which is to say every morning I lived in that room on the third floor, I felt I was in exactly the right place, which is rare for someone as distractible as me. At the end of each day, as the mosquitoes were starting to buzz, I would close it, pausing first to peer out at the orange sun sinking, listening for the call to prayer from the storefront mosque across the field.

All that happened, cold mornings barefoot on the marble around temple, lunch time tiffins of crunchy Bengali fish, my son's afternoon baths in an orange bucket in the sun, early evening walks along the grey river bed, these were the blocks of daily life. The bathroom window was just on the sideline of necessity. And yet, the bathroom window is what mattered, somehow, as much as everything else, if not more. The window began and ended each day. It was how I would determine the weather, the fog, the need for a hat. Its function was its beauty. Looking through it, even looking at it from across the room—looking at the window and knowing that through it, on the other side, was the rice paddy, the sun, and the green and white makeshift minarets whose loud speakers paced the rhythm of my days—provided the whole world, but in a small enough, square enough shape, so that I fit right in, too.  ✧

# THEATRE

## POST ROAD

## the false sun recordings

At a time of extraordinary displacement and global confusion,
these insistently sane poems manage a remarkable interaction of viable
realities, of multiple twists, turns and provisions of language's singular
instrument, syntax, and the words which it puts in order. Each turn here
is a possibility, an endlessly refracting multiplicity of instances.
Each word takes its own step, as it must, toward recognition.
        —*Robert Creeley*

# Scenes From the Life & Times of Little Billy Liver

Dennis DiClaudio

## Characters:

Catherine Rogers: Billy's mother, a tired working class woman.

Burt "Big Cat" Carter: A lonely truck-driving man.

Mr. Gazarian: A kindly gas station owner.

Victor Greenman: A slick L.A. talent agent.

Deborah Leiberthal: An attractive Hollywood photographer and starfucker.

Kyle Mann: A small-time film actor, looking for his break.

Little Billy Liver: A liver.

## Episode 1:

*LITTLE BILLY LIVER, young, impressionable and eager, sits quietly in the kitchen, taking in the last moments of his boyhood, while his mother, CATHERINE ROGERS, sullenly watches the rain streak against the window pane.*

CATHERINE: I suppose that I always knew that this day would come. Eventually. But, I never wanted to believe it. Belief is a funny thing, Billy. Like our hearts and our heads don't have to work together at the same time. Like they were never meant to. You can know a thing and not believe it. And you can believe something with all your heart and know at the same time that it isn't so. Like your heart and your head are fighting for your . . . your . . . your being. And the funny thing is that they're both right about half of the time.

 When you were born, the doctors said you wouldn't live. You couldn't live. It was impossible. They knew. A person can't survive without a heart or a head, or lungs, kidneys, a pancreas, a stomach, a digestive tract, a nervous system, lungs, kidneys, a spinal chord, a nose, ears, lungs, legs, arms, fingers, skin. They said a baby born with just a liver had no chance for survival. They knew. They were men of intelligence. Of education, with their books and their stethoscopes and their diplomas on the wall. They knew. And I knew. I knew they were right. But I never *believed* them.

 I always told you that you could do anything you wanted. I never wanted you to feel deprived of the opportunities that other children had. Or wanted you to think that the world was less wide for you. I told you that you were not less of a person than the boys who played football and climbed trees. What you lacked in extremities and organs, you more than made up for in potential. You were special. You *are* special. I believed it. And I know it. But, today, I wish I'd never told you.

*(She breaks into tears.)*

I'm sorry. Aren't I allowed to be a little selfish today? Can't I cry on the day that I lose my little boy? When you walk out that door, you're not a boy anymore. You're a man. I worked so hard so that this day could come, but now that it's here I wish it would never come. I wish that you would just stay my little boy.

*(She regains her composure and places a suitcase by Billy's chair.)*

I packed all of your things, or at least what you'll need. And I made you a lunch.

*(She tenderly wraps a scarf around Billy and places a rain cap on top of him.)*

There's five-hundred dollars in here. It's not much, but it will get you started. I've been putting away, little by little, for years. Because I knew this day would come. I knew.

*(Black out.)*


### Episode 2:

*Billy sits in the passenger seat of a large truck, travelling down a dark and lonely stretch of highway. BURT "BIG CAT" CARTER sits at the wheel.*

BIG CAT: Burt Carter. Big Cat. You see? That's how I got the handle. Because of the initials. It's important for a man on the road to have a handle. Without a handle, a man's anonymous. And the one thing a man can't be is anonymous, not on the road. You go crazy. You sit inside yourself. This radio full of voices keeps you sane. It's just voices, but it keeps you sane.

You got a handle, kid? We should give you a handle. Let's see.

*(He looks Billy up and down, sizing him up.)*

You ain't too big, but that don't matter. Little something. No hair. Can't call you Little Blondy or Little Blacky. Already a Little Blacky, and you don't want his name. Fella outta Fresno. Stayed awake for eighty-nine hours on pills and coke and then crashed his rig into a battalion of boyscouts in the desert. Doing four-to-twelve in the house. Listen, you stay away from that stuff. That ain't nothing but trouble. Believe me. I seen it all. I seen it all. Or at least most of it.

A man sees a lot on the road. Sometimes the road is all a truck-driving man really knows. I sometimes liken myself to a lonely sailor out at sea. The road is the ocean, and this truck is my ship. The road is powerful strong. It's long and wide and stretches out as far as you can see. And when the sun rises over it, it looks like it's made of gold. A force of nature.

It gives life and it takes it back. You gotta respect a force of nature. But, you gotta fear it at the same time. There are countless ghosts on this road, and you can hear them all through this radio. That's why a man needs a handle. So he can talk to the other ghosts.

*(He slaps his hands together in revelation.)*

Little Billy Liver! That's it! That's your handle! Little Billy Liver. Suits you, don't you think?

*(They stare out at the road before them.)*

Sure is nice to have someone to talk to.

*(Black out.)*


## Episode 3:

*Billy sits in the office of a dirty roadside gas station. His boss, MR. GAZARIAN, sits across from him.*

MR. GAZARIAN: Sit down, Billy. Make yourself comfortable. Now, Billy, the reason I asked you in here is . . . Goddamnit, this is gonna be hard for me to say. I've always thought of you as a son, Billy. You know that. My own son, he died over there in the Gulf. It's a sad act of the world that he died defending the very oil that I made my living from. Distilled down to gasoline and pumped into the gas tanks of BMWs heading westward down the interstate. Stockbrokers on vacation, looking for America. They don't know America. You can look out your back door and see America.

*(He brings his hand to his eyes to hide the tears.)*

I knew this would be hard.

Billy, I'm going to have to let you go. Now, you know it's nothing personal. You know that. You're a hard worker. You do your best. You do your best. It's just not working out.

When you showed up at my station, a scruffy kid, covered in the dust of the road, looking for a place to spend the night, I could see a spark in your . . . Well, I could tell you had a fire in you. You were out looking for life, and you needed a break. So, I gave you a chance and a job, a cot in the back. 'Cause I wanted to help you to get to wherever it was that you were going. But, that was six months . . .

Goddamnit! A person needs arms and legs to pump gas! That's just the way it is. I don't make the rules.

It's not your fault. I always liked you, Billy. Like a son. I know it's not fair. But, who ever said that life is supposed to be fair, goddamnit?! You think I wanted to spend my Fourth of Julys laying flowers in a military graveyard? Is that fair?

I'm sorry. I guess what I'm getting at is, sometimes life has things planned for us and we can't get around them. Like, I was meant to sell gasoline to cityfolk on the interstate. And my boy was meant to die in some country that he'd never even heard of six months before. And you, you Billy, you were meant for something much much more. I don't know what life has waiting for you, but I know it's big. Bigger than sleeping in the stockroom of some sad old man's gas station.

The worst thing in the world is wasted life. And you've got so much life in you. You don't have to believe me, but I'm doing this for you.

I want you to pack up your things and leave. You're fired.

*(Black out.)*

## Episode 4:

*Billy sits with a shot and a beer in a small town honky-tonk. His guitar is at his side. VICTOR GREENMAN, in an expensive suit, clearly not dressed for this joint, approaches. Sad, drinking country music plays on the jukebox.*

GREENMAN: Is this seat taken? Can I sit?

*(He sits without waiting for a response.)*

Can I buy you a drink? You okay? Okay, fine.

That was some performance. I'm really impressed. Really. Little Billy Liver. That's a catchy stage name. Would look real nice on a CD. I'm just speculating now. I mean, know no one really knows the industry. I mean *knows* knows the industry. Some people know better than others, but no one really *knows.*

*(He extends his hand to Billy.)*

Victor Greenman. I'm a talent agent. Los Angeles. That's the city of angels.

*(Having received no response, he pulls back his hand.)*

You're skeptical. That's smart. I can tell you're smart. That's what I like about you. It come out in your music. You're not like these flash-in-the-pan pop singers with their jeans down to their ass-cracks. Not that I haven't made a lot of money off those kids. I can't complain. They bought me the car that I have in the parking lot. Ferrari. And this suit. Georgio Armani. I'll tell you one thing. When I stepped into this place to get direction to Vegas, I sure as shit didn't expect to see what I saw. Or hear what I heard. Like I was saying before, some people know the industry better than others. But nobody knows the industry like me. And, when I see talent, I can taste it. And you taste like a million bucks.

*(He slides his business card across the table to Billy and then stands.)*

Think of it this way, talent is a gift from God. It makes people happy. And you could be making a lot of people happy. Is there anything better than that? Think about it.

*(He walks off. Black out.)*

**Episode 5:**

*Billy sits in a photography studio wearing a rhinestone cowboy hat, with his guitar at his side. DEBORAH LEIBERTHAL, photographer to the stars, circles him, snapping pictures.*

DEBORAH: That's it. That's it. Give me pain. Give me grit. Show me the black spot on your soul. That's what women want. That's what women want to fuck. They want to fuck that darkness. And men too. And dogs and cats and cars and microphones and cameras. The fucking sun wants to fuck the darkness. It's drawn to it. It wants to stick its big bright sunbeam dick into that dark hole. That's what sex is all about. That's why one amoeba first climbed onto another amoeba. For the pain of it all. Sex is pain. Pain is death, and sex is sex.

You've got the pain in you. It's where the brilliance lives. Artists who are happy aren't artists. They're busboys. Oh, that's beautiful.
*(She stops to reload her camera.)*
You're a very photogenic subject. You know that? You know it. You don't fool me for a millisecond with that good ol' country boy act.
*(She starts snapping pictures again.)*
I've photographed a thousand people. Men and women. And I can tell who has the pain 'cause they make my pussy wet. And when my pussy gets wet, I know it's 'cause I'm sitting on twenty-four-carat gold.

You know what? Music doesn't sell records. Or movie tickets. Or washing machines. I've worked with the greats. I've shot them and hung them on my wall. And you know what? Do you want to know what they all had in common? You know what you have in common? I can see it. And I know how to put it on the page. You can be so fucking huge. And I can make it happen.
*(She pulls Billy's hat from him and puts it on her own head.)*
So, what say we take some . . . private photographs?
*(She drops to her knees and leans in to kiss him. Black out.)*

**Episode 6:**

*Billy reclines in a sleazy hotel bed partially concealed by a sheet. KYLE MANN, a struggling film actor, also in half-dress, strokes at Billy's guitar and sings Billy's own words back to him.*

KYLE: *(singing)*
*Nobody loves you*
*And you ain't got no flesh and bone*
*Can't bring yourself to cry*

*When you're lying all alone*
*Can't figure out why*
*You're doin' all you can*
*It don't come to nothin'*
*You're not even half a man.*

When I'm lying by myself, listening to you, to your music, I know it's stupid, but I feel like you're singing just to me. Like you know somehow without ever having met me. Like you know some universal truth.

When you wrote that song, did you imagine someone like me? How can you understand me when you don't even know me. Well, know me know me. *(laughs a bit)*

I'm being stupid. I mean, obviously, you didn't write that for me. Not just for me.

(He lays back and strokes Billy tenderly, playfully.)

I've never done this before. I'm glad I met you at that party. I'm glad I waited for you. But this is all new for me. But it feels. Well, it feels . . . I don't know Billy. There's something about you. This is so fucked up. I don't like men. I mean, I like you. But, you're not a man, are you? You're something more. You're . . .

Christ, if I could only get some of what you have. Because I sure as hell don't have it. Not me. God spooned that out at the beginning, and you can tell he played favorites. For ten years, I've been playing the game in this city—auditions and auditions and auditions—and I don't know how much longer I can go on with it. I mean, at what point do you have to look yourself in the mirror and tell yourself that it's time to go back to Iowa. Iowa. The boys in Iowa would never believe this.

Why do I keep it up? I think it's people like you. Not that I'm blaming you. Not at all. I'm to blame. Do you think a moth wants to be a light bulb? How do you think he feels when he gets his wings burned? The sadness is probably worse than the pain. Don't you think? Oh, how would you know. I'm sorry. I'm being stupid again. You should tell me to shut up.

Why are you being so quiet? *(pause)* I'm sorry. I'm embarrassing myself. *(He stands and starts grabbing his clothes from the floor.)*

I'm leaving. I'm sorry. I'm sorry. I didn't mean to . . . I just wanted. I guess I just wanted to . . . I'm sorry.

*(He starts for the door, but stops and looks back for a reaction from Billy. He gets none.)*

Don't worry. I won't tell anyone about this. A shame though. My wife would really get a kick.

*(He exits. Black out.)*

**Episode 7:**

*Billy lies drunk, half passed out, on the floor of his dressing room amid empty bottles of booze and pills. Just beneath him is a piece of white paper. Victor Greenman enters, appalled at the sight before him, and paces a bit before speaking.*

GREENMAN: Little Billy Liver. The darling of the music industry. *(kicks a bottle)* I think there's still a few drops left in that one.

This can't be good for you. I mean ... Well, you know. I don't have to say it. You're killing yourself. Why? A little bad press? Some compromising photos? Some fag actor's lurid tabloid story? You'll pull out of it. These things don't kill a career.

But that's not it, is it? I should've known when I met you. You've been heading down this path all along. Since the first. Well, I won't have it. I won't stand by and watch another one step off the ledge. I take your money. I make my living from you. But I won't pull the trigger. I'm dropping you from my agency. I just can't handle the responsibility.

What? Don't you have anything to say for yourself? What's this? *(grabs paper)* A suicide note? Funny, if you put this to music, it'd probably sell a million ... *(reads)*

I'm sorry, Billy. I'm sorry. Was your mother a good woman? Stupid question. My condolences. I'll send flowers. I'll sign your name on the card. I'm sure she would have liked that. But it doesn't change anything. You can chase your mother into the ground full time now. I wash my hands.

I will never understand you people. Luckily, I don't have to.

*(He walks out. Black out.)*


**Episode 8:**

*Billy sits on a street corner, panhandling. Burt "Big Cat" Carter happens past him on the street. Stops, looks back with recognition.*

BIG CAT: Billy? Little Billy Liver, is that you? My God, what happened to you? It's me. Big Cat. Big Cat Carter. I'm gonna get you out of here.

This isn't a place for you. Out here with the whores and pump freaks. Oh, Billy. You let the road slip out from beneath your tires. Lucky for you I came along. I'm pulling a load down to Santa Fe. I'll give you ride. Get you back to someplace decent. Someplace where you belong. You don't belong here. This is no place for a little liver like you.

You gotta remember, Billy, you're gonna make some wrong turns, get some bad directions, but you can always get back on the turnpike at the next ramp.

*(He carries Billy offstage. Black out.)*

**Episode 9:**

*Billy sits in Mr. Gazarian's office once again. Gazarian stares out the back window.*

MR. GAZARIAN: *(His voice is gruff)* Billy . . . I've still got your cot made up in the back.
    *(He turns to Billy and smiles warmly. Pause. Black out.)*


The End   ✧

# CRITICISM

POST ROAD

Angela Ball
Frederick Barthelme
Steven Barthelme
David Berry
Mary Robison

Join us in Mississippi, where the workshops are tough, the people are friendly and entertaining, the affection leans toward genuine. We have three dozen writers working toward master's and doctoral degrees in fiction and poetry. We have visitors such as Rick Moody, Amy Hempel, Lucie Brock-Broido, Dana Gioia, Padgett Powell, Michael Waters, Mary Gaitskill, Julia Slavin, C. Michael Curtis and others. Recent graduates have won The Whiting Award, The Transatlantic Award, The *Playboy* Fiction Contest, and The Flannery O'Connor Award and have published widely. Six graduates published books with major publishers last year. We edit the *Mississippi Review* online and in paper, publish a student magazine, and manage to help our writers become better writers. For information, contact Rie Fortenberry at rief@mississippireview.com, check *www.centerforwriters.com*, or write us in that old fashioned way.

## THE CENTER FOR WRITERS

THE UNIVERSITY OF SOUTHERN MISSISSIPPI, BOX 5144, HATTIESBURG, MS 39406 (AA/EOE/ADAI)

# Streetstyle: Skateboarding, Spatial Appropriation, and Dissent

Taro Nettleton

Los Angeles may be planned or designed in a very fragmentary sense . . .
but it is infinitely envisioned.

*—Mike Davis,* City of Quartz

If Los Angeles needed to be imagined prior to its existence, as Mike Davis contends in *City of Quartz*, the same might be said of skateboarding. Historically, Los Angeles was a mirage in the desert whose existence depended upon the realization of a fantasy to see water in its arid landscape. Likewise, skateboarding in its initial stages—as a byproduct of another, paradigmatically Southern Californian youth-subculture, surfing—was premised on the ability of its inventors to imagine water in concrete. Skateboarding was born out of a desire to see concrete waves in the seemingly endless, concrete-laid Californian suburban sprawl.

Skateboarding's initially close ties to surf culture is revealed in its now largely retired alias, "sidewalk surfing." Surfing was and continues to be popularly understood as a benign subcultural pastime. As Rayner Banham explains in his *Los Angeles: The Architecture of Four Ecologies*, surfing may be understood as one of a particularly Californian brand of "private and harmless gratifications."[1] Surfing's perceived innocuousness is partly the result of a tacit understanding that any danger surfing poses—such as drowning, impalation on coral reefs, shark attacks—will only ever be suffered by the surfer. Surfing also works perfectly within the foundational myths that helped the initial waves of massive immigration to California: the cults of the body, health, and sun. According to these myths, the same climate conditions that bred "taller, broader-shouldered, thicker chested" college girls would have comparable effects on surfer boys.[2]

Through the mainstream success enjoyed by films such as John Milius's cult classic, *Big Wednesday* (1978), and musicians such as Dick Dale, Jan and Dean, and the Beach Boys,[3] the image of the surfer boy projected itself everywhere, producing enduring images of sunny southern California and exporting the surfer identity to be freely taken on even in places which had no access to waves.

---

[1] *Reyner Banham,* Los Angeles: The Architecture of Four Ecologies *(Berkeley: University of California, 1971) 111.*

[2] *Dr. David Starr Jordan quoted in Carey McWilliams,* Southern California: An Island on the Land *(Santa Barbara: Peregrine Smith, 1979) 110.*

[3] *The Beach Boys, of course, did not surf, but this was a minor qualification of their image that did not hinder their musical success.*

In spite of its historical ties to surfing, skateboarding enjoyed none of its predecessor's luck. To borrow Mike Davis' dialectical characterization of Los Angeles, skateboarding can be seen as the "noir" counterpart to surfing's "sunshine." The primitiveness of the violence out of which skateboards were born was of an entirely different order than the innocently primitive spirituality that drove surfboard shapers. The birth of the skateboard was characterized by a kind of primitiveness that civilization would prefer to leave behind. Yet surfboard "shaping"—the attempt to fashion the smoothest possible surface out of wood, and later fiberglass—was equated with spiritual pursuit despite its obvious emphasis on surface. Consequently the search for perfectly smooth surfaces was incorporated into the works of artists such as John McCracken[4] and celebrated as a part of a definitive L.A. aesthetic. The skateboard, on the other hand, as Jay "Boy" Adams, a cult icon and veteran of professional skateboarding puts it, "was based on tearing apart rollerskates."

Fairly early on in its history[5], skateboarding got a *Life* magazine cover story, in the May 14, 1965 issue entitled "Skateboard Mania—and Menace." This story finds itself amidst other cultural-interest articles such as "see through Sweaters—knitwear joins the trend on nudity," and "Space-Walk—Cosmonaut's Story." The generally hostile tone of the article is established in the first sentence—"That thing 19 year-old Pat McGee is balancing on is a skateboard, the most exhilarating and dangerous joyriding device this side of the hot rod." Skateboarding is hastily set up through the evocation of hot-rod culture as a form of juvenile delinquency, both dangerous and despicable (in the figure of Ed Roth, who provided graphics for skateboard decks as well as kustom kar designs, this parallel was very real). The perceived death wish of skateboarders is emphasized in one of the call-outs of the article—"It's easier to get bloody than fancy"—and an accompanying photograph of a mangled foot. More akin to a warning against an infectious virus than a journalistic report, the article is littered with hospital statistics and other tales of injuries. One caption, referring to the mother of a skateboarder who decided to try it for herself, reads as follows:

> It reminded Mrs. Greer of a roller coaster and gave her "a very free kind of feeling, but if Peter had let go of me, I think I would have died." She was luckier than a California woman who tried her son's board and got going too fast. He landed on both elbows and now has one arm in a sling, the other in a cast.

---

[4] See Sunshine and Noir: Art in L.A., *1960-1997 (Humlebaek, Denmark: Louisiana Museum of ModernArt, 1997).*

[5] *Skateboards started to be produced commercially around 1959, according to Michael Brooke. See* Concrete Wave: The History of Skateboarding *(Toronto, Canada: Warwick, 1999).*

But what is it exactly about skateboarding that strikes such a nerve for its reporter, and presumably for the readers of *Life* magazine? As in surfing, the injuries, even according to this paranoid article, are sustained exclusively by those doing the skateboarding. Or as it was put by Bob Muller, a native Californian in a letter to the editor published three weeks later, "so what if we get a few broken bones, scraped knees and lumpy heads.[6] They're our bones, knees and heads." Despite Muller's rebuttal, by August 1965 skateboarding was banned from the streets and sidewalks of twenty U.S. cities.[7]

The disproportionate alarm caused by skateboarding in comparison to surfing has to do with the space in which it is practiced. Limited to water, surfing is always kept at bay. Because surfing is relegated to the beach and the water, which ultimately are spaces of leisure, surfing poses no threat to the limits of prescribed spatial use. Skateboarding, on the other hand, brings itself onto the land, and thus positions itself within the complex delineations of public and private space. Because the functionality of suburban spaces is premised on the clear definition of public and private space, skateboarding is seen as an irritant. By reconceptualizing the concrete as water, skateboarders threw sand into the lubricant necessary for the city's and the suburbs' smooth operation.

Marxist spatial theorist Henri Lefebvre asserts that "private space is distinct from, but always connected with, public space" and "in the best of circumstances, the outside space of the community is dominated, while the indoor space of family life is appropriated."[8] Skateboarding may be said to use the already confused delimitation between public and private to its own advantage. It appropriates so-called public spaces that are in reality increasingly dominated by privatization. For those who are invested in—and profit from—the rigidly administered uses of space such as the strip mall, skateboarding is indeed a nuisance. It both creates and functions as "noise" in its interference in commerce. In their alternate use of the strip mall, for instance, a space which is ambiguously both open to the public and designed with a single, non-civic purpose in mind, skateboarders become an unwanted presence precisely for their refusal to take part in consumption, and for obfuscating the architecturally articulated boundaries of permissible and prohibited use.

In the 1970s, skateboarders found an answer to their search for transitions from a horizontal to vertical plane. The ultimate concrete wave was in the absence of water—in swimming pools, drain pipes, ditches, and dried-up aqueducts. Rejoicing in the desiccation of the lifelines of L.A.,[9]—and pools, which would frequently be emptied as a result of the

[6] *"Skateboard Mania—and Menace,"* Life *4 June, 1965.*

[7] *Brooke, 24.*

[8] Henri Lefebvre, The Production of Space *(Cambridge: Blackwell, 1991) 166.*

[9] *Carey McWilliams,* Southern California: An Island on the Land *(Santa Barbara: Peregrine Smith, 1979) 183. McWilliams writes: "Water is the life-blood of Southern California."*

frequent fires in the Hollywood Hills and Santa Monica Mountains[10]—
the practice of skateboarding took on a distinctly noir tinge, negatively
criticizing and emphasizing the ecological instability of L.A.[11] The trans-
gressiveness of the skateboarders' gestures registered both symbolically
and judicially, as trespassing was often necessary to access desirable sites.
In disregarding the very concept of private property by entering backyards,
skateboarders parodied the concept of indoor/outdoor living, a paradigmatically Californian lifestyle and architectural metaphor. Furthermore,
skateboarders critiqued the ideological premise of suburban life—
community living realized through increased privacy, seclusion, and
exclusion—by literally bringing themselves from outside in.

As contemporary spatial theorist Iain Borden points out, in
Lefebvreian terms, this mode of skateboarding remains in the realm of
co-optation, rather than appropriation.[12] For Lefebvre, the difference
between the two concepts is marked by temporality and power and is
hence parallel to French sociologist and theorist Michel de Certeau's distinction between "strategies" and "tactics." De Certeau defines strategies
as "the calculus of force relationships" that can be taken by "subject[s] of
will and power (a proprietor, an enterprise, a city, a scientific institution)."[13]
Tactics, on the other hand, are used by those who lack both institutionalized
power and a proper place "where [tactics] can capitalize on its advan-
tages, prepare its expansions, and secure independence with respect to
circumstances."[14]

To illustrate the distinction between co-optation and appropriation,
Lefebvre cites "Christianity's co-optation of the Roman basilica,"[15] going
on to state that for its co-optation, the space had to be consecrated. Thus
co-optation requires power for its implementation and supposes a rela-
tive permanence of control. In Borden's words, co-optation differs from
appropriation in its lack of ephemerality.[16] Skateboarders were deprived
of the means for administrating spaces; the occupation of spaces such as
pools and pipes could always only be temporary. These spaces could only
be appropriated until the law appeared. The limited effectiveness of the
attempted co-optation by skateboarders can be seen, then, as a result of

---

[10] *Iain Borden*, Skateboarding, Space and the City: Architecture and the Body *(New York: Berg, 2001) 47.*

[11] *For an apocalyptic account of the ecological instability of Los Angeles, see Mike Davis,* Ecology of Fear *(New York: Metropolitan, 1998).*

[12] *Borden, 55.*

[13] *Michel de Certeau, introduction,* The Practice of Everyday Life *(Berkeley: University of California, 1984) xix.*

[14] *Ibid.*

[15] *Lefebvre, 369.*

[16] *Borden, 47.*

their deployment of strategic rather than tactical means. As de Certeau writes, "a strategy assumes a place that can be circumscribed as proper . . . The 'proper' is a victory of space over time."[17]

However, by defining their practices in mere opposition to dominant spatial practices, pool skaters failed to fundamentally negotiate the structure which makes spatial domination possible. As a result, in many pools skateboarders attempted to rewrite spatiality in their own names through the application of graffiti—in effect replicating the desire for spatial mastery. The natural extension of this trajectory was the imagining and the production of skateparks, and backyard halfpipes, which offered themselves as utopian oases. Due to their large scale, these spaces were often separated from everyday life. *Bones Brigade Video III: The Search for Animal Chin* (1987) was then the largest scale skate video production to date. It is produced by then leading skateboard manufacturer Powell-Peralta and, as all skateboard videos do, it serves as a promotional video of the professionals they sponsor. Ostensibly in search of a mythical figure named Animal Chin, the Bones Brigade's search leads them to an enormous halfpipe named the Chin Ramp located in the middle of a barren desert. In its giant scale, minimalist/functionalist aesthetics, and location within a "rugged nature,"[18] the Chin Ramp closely resembles the modernist architectural aesthetic of "the machine in the garden"—or the desert, as is the case here.

Of course, such structures were necessarily un-urban, and more often than not privately owned, or built as a part of a film set, as is the case above. In their monumentality and singularly defined purpose, such purely functional structures managed to elide a connection to their spatial context, successfully sanitizing the sport of its appropriational nature. It was in these terms that skateboarding achieved an unprecedented mass popularity.

Later on, in the 1980s and 1990s, with its return to the streets, skateboarding was increasingly articulated in tactical terms. In its most recent and currently most popular incarnation, skateboarding happens in the downtown center. An exploration of this performance of the city offers insights into the production of "downtown" as social space by giving us an example of spatial dissent. While street skating is a global phenomenon, and certainly not limited to downtown L.A., the skateboarding industry remains centered in California, and—like Hollywood cinema—the visual ephemera produced by the industry, both in print and video, disseminate images of southern California and situates it as its paradigmatic landscape. Like potential actors, many aspiring professional skateboarders

---

[17] *de Certeau, xix..*

[18] *Thomas S. Hines, "Machines in the Garden: Notes Toward a History of Modern Los Angeles Architecture, 1900-1990,"* Sex, Death, and God in L.A., *ed. David Reid (Berkeley: University of California, 1994) 287.*

flock to California for a chance to be "discovered." Likewise, many skateboarders (myself included) visit seeming "non-places" that are nevertheless mythologized in skateboard videos, such as the convex curbs on Venice beach or the curb that wraps around a Safeway supermarket in San Francisco.

So what does streetstyle skateboarding offer in terms of understanding the city? First and foremost, it shows us that there are sidewalks. In *City of Quartz*, Mike Davis criticizes Marxist critic Frederic Jameson and architect Frank Gehry for their "giddy" postmodernist stance and for taking an aerial view in place of a pedestrian or street level perspective of the effects of downtown "revitalization" in L.A. In regard to Jameson's famous account of the Bonaventure hotel, Davis writes:

> What is missing from Jameson's [description] . . . is the savagery of [the Bonaventure's] insertion into the surrounding city . . . to speak of its "popular" character is to miss the point of its systematic segregation from the great Hispanic-Asian city outside.[19]

Gehry fairs even worse. Davis characterizes his portfolio as "a mercenary celebration of bourgeois-decadent minimalism."[20] While Davis argues that Jameson and Gehry respectively ignore and produce the militarization of downtown, and consequently turn a blind eye to any cultural activity outside of finance and commerce in the downtown area, his own recourse to a "thriving Latino culture"[21] in this respect remains largely amorphous and parenthetical. Despite his intention—that is presumably for a proletarian revolution of L.A.—he leaves little room for any counter-hegemonic articulation.

Davis suggests that the fortress architecture of downtown L.A. is a result of the peripheralization of industry and the centralization of finance capital, an effect of class polarization resulting from the development of capitalism. I want to suggest that offering such conclusions without any alternatives has the effect of gridlocking any possible counter-cultural activity. It is in lieu of such an impression that I want to posit the activity of streetstyle skateboarding.

It is significant that skateboarders in many downtowns flock specifically to spaces that are modeled after Rockefeller Center. Of these spaces, Davis writes, quoting Italian Marxist architectural critic Manfredo Tafuri: "the final development for the plan was 'a contained and rational concentration, an oases of order—a closed and circum-

---

[19] Mike Davis, "Urban Renaissance and the Spirit of Postmodernism," Postmodernism and its Discontents: Theories, Practices, ed. E. Ann Kaplan (New York: Verso, 1988) 86.

[20] Davis, City of Quartz (New York, Vintage, 1992) 236.

[21] Davis, City of Quartz 231.

scribed intervention.'"[22] Davis situates the Rockefeller Center model as the genealogical precursor to the Bonaventure hotel. As such, he sees it as giving rise to a new architectural ideology which "redefined [genuine public spaces] as planning problems to be eliminated or privatized."[23] Yet for skateboarders, these apparently hostile spaces which resist unsolicited occupation are "the places to be." It may be useful to consider the viewpoint of Jesse Neuhaus, a former professional skateboarder, on these structures: "the corporate types see their structures as powerful and strong . . . I see them as something I can enjoy, something I can manipulate to my own advantage."[24]

More specifically, streetstyle skateboarding privileges non-places of architectural punctuation such as landscaping, planters, curb cuts, and parking lots. In doing so, this practice engages in poetic misuses of non-places. These non-places also constitute "a series of opportunity constraints," effected by architectural boundaries, or "vertical planes preventing horizontal movement across the city."[25] Boundaries such as walls, ledges, barriers, and handrails are also the foundational elements of downtown architecture. As French critic Michel de Certeau suggests about these borders:

> Everything refers in fact to this differentiation which makes possible the isolation and interplay of distinct spaces. From the distinction that separates a subject from its exteriority to the distinctions that localize objects, from the home (constituted on the basis of a wall) to the journey (constituted on a the basis of a geographical "elsewhere" or a cosmological "beyond"), from the functioning of an urban network to that of rural landscape, there is no spatiality that is not organized by the determination of frontiers. [26]

At the same time that these elements define the space that they surround, their infrastructural role remains largely ignored. It is through the presumed architectural insignificance of these boundaries that an illusion of freedom and mobility are expressed to the inhabitants of city space.

In the city, street skaters highlight the existence of boundaries, which are designed to be disregarded, by grinding them down, and transgressing them at will. Street skating irrevocably brings these architectural boundaries into visibility, not only calling attention to them by skate-

---

[22] Davis, "Urban Renaissance," 84.

[23] Davis, "Urban Renaissance," 85.

[24] Leah Garchik, "The Urban Landscape," reprinted from San Francisco Chronicle (1994) at http://web.cps.msu.edu/~dunhamda/dw/urban.html.

[25] Iain Borden, "Boundaries," City A-Z, ed. Steve Pile & Nigel Thrift (New York: Routledge, 2000) 21.

[26] de Certeau, The Practice of Everyday Life (Berkeley: University of California, 1984) 123.

boarding on them, but also by encouraging the owners of these private or municipal boundaries to respond by installing architectural devices.[27] These devices are equivalent to the third armrest on "bumproof" benches and sprinklers installed in parks to prohibit potential sleepers,[28] except for the additional fact that they serve no function whatsoever other than that of prohibition. Like paint used to cover up graffiti that fails to match the original color of the wall, these contraptions suggest a level of absurdity by putting little walls on top of bigger walls, in the end simply calling explicit attention to a helpless desire for control. In this way, street skating exposes the contradictory and schizophrenic nature of the way in which public and private spaces of downtowns are articulated.

The increasing deployment of such prohibitive structures in downtown areas, and a concurrent resurgence of legislative actions to ban skateboarding from streets and plazas—and to restrict its practice to public skateboard parks, "where the action is radical but lacks the inspiration of a knock-down, drag-out backyard pool session or a skate cruise down the boulevard with the crew"—has incited a proliferation of fiery responses.[29] Contemporary skateboard publications are filled with rhetoric urging skateboarders to stay in the streets and to "keep it real." In a section of a recent issue of *Thrasher* magazine that serves as a forum for reader-submitted photos, one caption reads as follows: "Benches, knobs ... they threw every anti-skate device in existence at Hubba. Guess what? IT'S STILL A SKATESPOT, FUCKERS!" At the bottom of the same photograph is a solicitation from "Skatespot Liberation Army" to "send in flicks of you using and abusing any and all skate-proof spots."[30] Even more explicitly, one skateboard manufacturer, Real Skateboards, ran an advertisement that doubles as a call to action:

> Now that everyone loves skateboarding and it's on every TV and cities are building parks everywhere it makes it even harder to skate in any downtown. The fake fuckers want skateboarding on their own terms, in their designated areas. Any street, anywhere is still off limits. Not anymore. The war is not over—Don't be seen but leave your mark.[31]

While much of the language used in these responses takes on a militaristic—and hence strategic—tone, skateboarders lack the means to realize strategic action. All of the actions called for remain on the level of

---

[27] *For examples, see "Ravensforge Skateboard Solutions": http://www.ravensforge.com/products.htm.*

[28] *Davis,* City of Quartz *233.*

[29] *Kevin Thatcher, "Grab that Board!" from the first issue of* Thrasher, *reprinted at http://web.cps.msu.edu/~dunhamda/dw/grab.html.*

[30] *"Photograffiti,"* Thrasher *Nov. 2001: 175.*

[31] Thrasher, *62.*

tactical subversion. In de Certeauian terms, the rhetoric urges skateboarders to "make do" with the available resources.

Therefore, skateboarding offers us a way in which the increasingly geometric space of the city can be negotiated so as to overlay "a poetic reading," which resists "proper" use and enacts resistance within the context of an architectural administration of power.[32] Through this imposition, what were formerly non-places are transformed into social spaces. Henri Lefebvre defines the latter as "both a field of action (offering its extension to the deployment of projects and practical intentions) and a basis of action (a set of places whence energies derive and whither energies are directed)."[33] By dialectically reading architecturally prohibitive elements as both fields and bases of action, and inserting an element of play into the architectural language of power, skateboarding perverts the humorlessly rigid delineations regulated by the grid of downtown.

I do not intend to fashion skateboarding as any sort of "way out," or to imbue it with explicitly political radicalism. Nevertheless, skateboarding does offer a narrative through which we can imagine an appropriation of the structures of control, and move toward what Lefebvre has called "the true space of pleasure, which would be an appropriated space par excellence, [which] does not yet exist."[34]  ✧

[32] de Certeau, 105.

[33] Lefebvre, The Production of Space (Cambridge: Blackwell, 1991) 191.

[34] Lefebvre, The Production of Space (Cambridge: Blackwell, 1991) 167.

# RECOMMENDATIONS  POST ROAD

# NOON

NOON

A LITERARY ANNUAL

1369 MADISON AVENUE   PMB 298
NEW YORK   NEW YORK   10128-0711

EDITION PRICE   $9 DOMESTIC   $14 FOREIGN

# AN AMERICAN MEMORY and I AM ZOE HANDKE by Eric Larsen

Virginia Holman

In 1988 and again in 1992, Eric Larsen published two of the most exquisitely rendered novels I have ever read: *An American Memory* and *I Am Zoe Handke*. The novels are surely most appreciated together, though each book has a voice and a story that resonates alone. On the surface, the two books seem to serve as the story of a marriage in much the same way as Evan Connell's *Mrs. Bridge* and *Mr. Bridge*. Connell's books are masterful in their portrait of estrangement and loneliness in America. Larsen's books, though they at first reveal detailed family histories that are dark and oppressive, show us how, sometimes, even the most psychologically damaged among us can build deep, sustaining, and loving relationships.

*An American Memory* is a collection of notebook entries written and ordered by Malcolm Reiner, the novel's protagonist, in a meticulous but desperate attempt to order and make meaning of his life, his father's life, and his grandfather's life. The book starts off as Malcolm conjures his memories of his severe Calvinist grandfather and begins ordering the details of his life and then the life of his father in desperate attempt to understand their struggles as Norwegian immigrants—the culture that to Malcolm felt as if it prized repression over passion and violent passion over love—a family where gentleness and trusting love was rarely found.

Malcolm is a profoundly quiet child and as such becomes a collector of sounds. He listens intently to the wind and snow, to gunshots, to the turning of pages in a book. Malcolm hears the tinkle of ice in a drink glass, glass smashing, and tables and doors being crushed under the weight of more than one man's burden.

Malcolm salvages enough of himself to begin gathering his memories together and eventually marrying the young Zoe Handke. The first novel ends early in the couple's marriage. Zoe (of *I Am Zoe Handke*) starts out more robust a young woman in comparison to Malcom's young man, and that's exactly the problem. Zoe, born at nineteen to a whippet thin mother, is despised, she thinks, for ruining her mother's life. Her mother's terrible rages that led her to tear her daughter's clothes, the fact that she seems to inhabit the lush body of a woman seems to spur Zoe's mother deeper into an unstoppable madness and institutionalizations.

Once Zoe leaves the home of her mother and its considerable pall, she spins dangerously close to madness herself, having lost her "place" as the recipient of her mother's rage. As Zoe begins to confront and try to make sense of her childhood, she finds that she cannot explore this terrain safely. Zoe exhibits symptoms of severe trauma, experiencing hysterical deafness and then blindness. Finally, she finds hope in the smallest memories, and finds that she has enough images of love and caring within her to build a relationship and, ultimately, a family.

Zoe writes, "I was born into my mother's madness." Her supreme accomplishment is that she is able to live a generative life in spite of it. Larsen is a naturalist and he does not spare his characters their punishing pasts. But hope lives here in these deeply fractured lives, and a desire to live, and love and intimacy, and the family that we make.

If you could read a Bergman film, say, *Wild Strawberries*, you would be reading Eric Larsen.  ✧

# WIND, SAND AND STARS by Antoine de Saint-Exupéry

Pete Hausler

Best known for his classic children's book *The Little Prince*, Antoine de Saint-Exupéry was also an accomplished novelist and memoirist. In fact, it could be argued that he was far more competent at writing than at the subject of most of his books: piloting airplanes. For a dozen-plus years preceding the outbreak of World War II, he was a commercial aviator, flying for the French courier company Aéropostale. He was stationed both in South America (flying the spine of the Andes through Chile and Argentina) and in French West Africa (navigating between Toulouse and such African cities as Dakar, Marrakech, Casablanca, and Cairo, and secluded military outposts in the Sahara). Sadly, in 1944 he disappeared without a trace while flying a war-related reconnaissance mission over the Mediterranean.

By most accounts, Saint-Exupéry was an average pilot, even after the benefit of the doubt given to aviators of that fledgling era. (An amusingly large number of his chapters begin with phrases like "A minor accident had forced me down.") But he possessed the inherent character traits of all pioneering airmen; namely, the can-do spirit of a Victorian explorer, and a sanguine and fatalistic acceptance of his dangerous job (like when he offhandedly mentions, "In those days our planes frequently fell apart in mid-air"). Throw in the heart of a philosopher-poet, and what results is the lyrical and sublime aviation narrative *Wind, Sand and Stars*.

Fans of *The Little Prince* will gain insight into that strange little book, by reading this strange little book. It wouldn't be too much of a stretch to say that *Wind, Sand and Stars* is the Ur-consciousness of *The Little Prince*, and its essence can be found in Wind: the little desert foxes, the plane crashes, the calm acceptance of an impending Saharan death, and finally, the thirst-induced hallucinations, during which Saint-Exupéry likely conjured his children's story.

For example, you can see the kernel of the very idea for Prince in the chapter, "The Plane and the Planet." Saint-Exupéry writes from the Sahara, atop "the flat top of the frustum of a cone, an isolated vestige of a plateau," where he had been forced down by some unnamed mechanical malady. Despite his dire situation, he takes great delight in supposing—probably correctly—that he is the first human to walk that particular plateau. While exploring his few acres of virgin sand, he kicks up a black rock and deduces—again probably correctly—that it is a small piece of meteorite. Further reconnoitering turns up a dozen similar stones, and this cosmic observation: "And here is where my adventure became magical, for in a striking foreshortening of time that embraced thousands of years, I had become the witness of this miserly rain from the stars."

When reading *Wind, Sand and Stars*, it helps to keep in mind the context. That is, its publication date was 1939, a time when most people had never flown in an airplane. Therefore a reader picking up this book fresh off the press most likely couldn't picture a river, or forest, or a desert, or mountains viewed from thousands of feet in the air. The power of Saint-Exupéry's description and rumination make maps animate. When, prior to his first courier flight, Saint-Exupéry asks a veteran pilot to give him some pointers on the route, "Guillaumet did not teach Spain to me, he made the country my friend." He speaks of three orange trees on the edge of a small town that are problematic when flying low. He describes a small, hidden brook west of the town of Motril, that "breaks up a whole field," and consequently earns the grudging compliment "that serpent in the grass." He chronicles an otherwise innocent, empty meadow where if he tried to land, "suddenly bang! there are thirty sheep in your wheels." The Spain thus described by Guillaumet, becomes to Saint-Exupéry "a sort of fairyland," where he marks on his map not only "the farmer, the thirty sheep, the brook," but also "a shepherdess forgotten by the geographers."

The most gripping chapters in *Wind* feature Saint-Exupéry describing the harrowing dangers faced by early aviators. These risks mostly involved crashing, and the subsequent extrication from hostile or barren landscapes. In the chapter, "The Men," Saint-Exupéry describes the miraculous self-rescue of Guillaumet, the above-mentioned mentor. Guillaumet's plane is brought down by stormy winter weather high in the Andes, and after five days of fruitless searching from the air by his fellow pilots, he's given up for dead. Seven days after disappearing, news comes that Guillaumet is indeed alive, that he has dragged his ill-clad and injured body over mountain peaks, in sub-zero temperatures, through fifteen-foot snow drifts until reaching a settlement. His first words to his friend Saint-Exupéry are: "I swear that what I went through, no animal would have gone through." From that point on, Guillaumet is elevated to status of demigod, and his tenacious joie de vivre runs as an inspirational thread throughout the rest of the author's own risky adventures and near-tragic mishaps.

One of those adventures is a breathtaking account of an afternoon-long battle to keep his plane in the air over the Andes, after being caught in hurricane-force winds. Saint-Exupéry modestly starts his account with the proclamation, "In beginning my story of a revolt of the elements . . . I have no feeling that I shall write something which you will find dramatic." This had me wondering if it was false modesty, for I have seldom read anything so dramatic as this thirteen-page depiction of man versus nature. The pacing is exquisite, near perfect. Saint-Exupéry manages to convey the acute sense of his sheer physical exhaustion during his prolonged fight, yet the description never feels overlong or exaggerated. And considering the seeming ease with which these early planes crashed and/or fell apart, you really have no idea if he will keep his plane aloft, or if it will be dashed into the side of a mountain and require a Guillaumet-type miracle escape.

Guillaumet's escape is invoked again in "Prisoners of the Sand," except this time it is Saint-Exupéry himself who defies death. While attempting a long-distance flight between Paris and Saigon, Saint-Exupéry drifts off-course over the Sahara, and an ensuing crash totals his plane. Miraculously, both he and his mechanic, Prévot, survive the crash virtually unscathed. However, they only have a quart of water, one orange, a few grapes, and a bit of cake. And to make matters worse, they have drifted so far from the intended flight path, they have little hope of rescue. What ensues is a trek in hopes of finding a desert outpost or oasis before the ravages of thirst and dehydration strike them down. Adding to the hardship is one dismal fact that Saint-Exupéry knows: under typical weather conditions, man can last approximately nineteen hours in the Sahara without water. A favorable, cooling wind initially prolongs their magical nineteen-hour window. After a day, however, the wind changes direction, normal weather conditions return, and clock starts ticking.

On the second night, Saint-Exupéry seemingly gives up; he digs a hole, covers himself with sand and calmly awaits death. In the morning, finding that he's still alive, he scrambles to his feet, his will to live restored, and admonishes his companion: "Our throats are still open. Get along, man!" By the third day, pilot and mechanic have each trekked an unbelievable 125 miles, on almost no water. Finally, when they start seeing spots in front of their eyes, when they have to rest every 200 yards, when they can no longer swallow from lack of saliva, when the delirium-induced mirages are nearly constant, salvation: "I had one last hallucination—three dogs chasing one another. Prévot looked, but could not see them. However, both of us waved our arms at a Bedouin." The Bedouin rescues them, and in gratitude, Saint-Exupéry addresses an earnest and eloquent coda to him:

> [Y]ou will dwell forever in my memory yet I shall never be able to recapture your features. You are Humanity and your face comes into my mind simply as man incarnate ... All my friends and all my enemies marched towards me in your person. It did not seem to me that you were rescuing me: rather did it seem that you were forgiving me. And I felt I had no enemy left in all the world.

It is these heart-warming paeans to his fellow Man, that keep *Wind, Sand and Stars* spinning. Pilots by their very nature are loners and Saint-Exupéry is no different. He clearly loves the solitude of the cockpit, where he can ruminate on man's place in the universe. And yet his glee in the company of humanity is ever-apparent. ✧

# Parts & Pieces: Sven Birkerts, A. Manette Ansay, Steve Stern, Christopher Tilghman, Elinor Lipman and Amy Hempel

Risa Miller

I actually freeze when someone asks me to recommend a book; I read like a writer and reading has gotten to feel so much like work that it's hard to read for pleasure and I'm always looking for reading palliatives, something that will give me a brain massage. I also follow the impulse of a certain yentakeit (Yiddish for *inquiring minds want to know*) and usually find myself reaching for biographies or memoirs.

So, the first book that comes to mind answers all these needs and explains how you become a world-class literary critic: Sven Birkerts's, *My Sky Blue Trades*, a memoir which comes as close as you can to "cracking the code" of family narrative. It's refreshingly counter-trend: you don't need horrific events, dysfunction, or addiction to provide emotional heft to personal evolution. And, of course, there are his extraordinary sentences. The truth is, as soon as I start mooning over one of Sven's sentences I take myself out of the palliative zone and try to figure out how he does what he does. Then, the reading becomes work again. It's as if the whole fades away and I start concentrating on the parts and the pieces and the writerly elements. I've worried that the concentration on parts and pieces is a psychopathology, but I've consoled myself that it's art, the same skewed way a cartoonist looks at a politician and sees a bulbous nose or elephant ears.

With parts and pieces and writerly elements in mind, here are some fiction recommendations: *Sister*, by A. Manette Ansay, a dense and symmetrical novel about how emotional past warps the emotional present. The structure and organization elude analysis; they're neither temporal, nor spatial, nor thematic, couldn't be outlined if you were paid to, yet I've taught the book to college freshmen who "get it" very quickly. Plus, this novel has a killer resonant last line.

*The Wedding Jester*, by Steve Stern, a collection of stories: there's no place I'd rather be than inside his acrobatic sentences, especially as his angels and dybbuks cross back and forth between worlds.

*In a Father's Place*, by Christopher Tilghman: the title story in this collection concerns a father whose adult children come home for a family weekend and give him the emotional heave-ho. Best in show and tell, without a single descriptive adverb—if I recall correctly. If there was one story for an emerging writer to read, this would be it.

Then there's Elinor Lipman, whose dialogue stuns and amazes. She holds up a tuning fork to a social wind and turns it into a Vivaldi concerto.

Just as amazing, her characters don't come off as irksome or smart-alecky. What comes to mind is the JA word (Jane Austen) which blurbers and critics love to throw around, but Elinor Lipman is the only real contender.

One more story collection, *Reasons to Live*, by Amy Hempel: full of bounce and step, yet there's scant exposition and it defies all conventions about a reader's need to be grounded. My favorite story, "In the Cemetery Where Al Jolson is Buried," apparently had a workshop kick-off: the assignment was to write about something you were ashamed of. So, it's about a hospital visit to a best friend dying of cancer. All that missing exposition turns out to be the power of the shame; what the narrator can't quite bring herself to explain is that, best friend or not, she'd rather be anywhere else in the world but that hospital room. The story reads as if it's written on onion skin paper and you have to lift it up to see what message the ink blots leave.

Did I mention palliative and yentakeit? One last thought: weekly picture magazines. I won't name them and I seldom buy them, but I pounce on them in the dentist's office and read as many as I can in the time it takes for one of my kids to get her teeth cleaned. Sometimes I get to the dentist's office early on purpose. ✧

# INSIDE THE SKY: A MEDITATION ON FLIGHT
## by William Langewiesche
# STICK AND RUDDER: AN EXPLANATION ON THE ART OF FLYING by Wolfgang Langewiesche

Maria Flook

I have had the pleasure of reading some nonfiction books by fathers and sons, and two of these father/son teams have had a resonating effect on my life as both reader and writer. Norman Maclean's tense and lyric masterpiece, *Young Men and Fire*, (University of Chicago Press, 1993, reissued), and his son John Maclean's *Fire on the Mountain*, (Wm. Morrow, 1999) when read back to back, gave me a wallop of the technical and romantic helix of fire fighting. In these books, the writers entered the terrain of both natural world disasters and the deadly bureaucratic boondoggles of fighting fires. The senior Maclean's book, *Young Men and Fire*, is probably the one to start with—and end with.

But the writers I want to talk about here are William Langewiesche and his father Wolfgang Langewiesche, both pilots, whose books about flight have informed my vision as a writer. Just as powerful and weirdly self-contained as the Macleans' tragic books about wild fires and fire fighters, in which philosophical thought and practical fact were often entwined, these two books about flying have had a sustaining philosophical meaning to me long after reading them. And the very rarified and quirky knowledge I have gained from these texts has, in fact, crept into my own work and has helped my goals as a realist.

William Langewiesche might be best known for his recent controversial book about the 911 clean-up, *American Ground: Unbuilding the World Trade Center* (Northpoint) in which he writes about "members of New York City's now sacrosanct Fire Department, who succumbed to greed and selfishness and divisiveness," (NYTBR), but I had first read William Langewiesche's nonfiction book, *Inside the Sky: A Meditation on Flight*. This book of distinctive essays not only examines recent air disasters such as the Valuejet crash in Florida, but along with its fascinating technical explanations, exposé and inquiry into modern aviation disasters and events, there are chapters about the interior experience, the human responses within the very exacting and always transforming "art of flying."

One early chapter introduces us to writer/socialist and naturalist, J. B. Jackson, who wrote about "landscape vernacular." Langewiesche writes, "'Vernacular' for Jackson meant the everyday evidence of people's ordinary lives, the way they really live them, as opposed to the way they are told they should." In this chapter he talks about seeing the world as a pilot from a cockpit and how one learns to recognize the "human vernacular" in the structures, highway grids and farmlands sweeping past below. He quotes Jackson, "It is from the air that the true relationship between the natural and the human landscape is first clearly revealed . . . The harmonious and intricate design of living and working on the face of the earth slowly evolves beneath us."

And in a chapter called "The Turn," Langewiesche writes about the upsetting but wholly practical strategy that allows huge jumbo jets to change direction and turn in a deep banking maneuver, how this process is as complex as it is simple—as all truths, whether in physics or dance, must meet at some connection point. His descriptions are lyric yet fully annotated and defined by fully graspable nuggets or correct science. His almost poetic description of a "gyroscope" of course gives complete instruction about its invention and practical use in aeronautics. His chapters on air disasters combine his acute understanding of the human grain with his scientific prowess in the step-by-step analyses of how mistakes happen, how perfect science and human error are always connected by a thread.

This book led me to the elder Langewiesche's wondrous work, *Stick and Rudder*, a text still considered to be the bible of aerial navigation. A seemingly much more "practical" guide to flying, this is a technical manual for first-time pilots with chapters entitled "How a Wing is Flown," "The Airplane's Gaits," "The Rudder," "The Glide," "The Approach," "The Landing Run," as well the charming title "Thin Air." The wonderful diction in these pages is my favorite mix of practical mechanics delivered in an authoritative colloquial, always masculine, but constantly elegant narrative. Facts, warnings, anecdotes, caveats, give guidance to the reader and the enticement to succeed. I will never get behind a stick, but I am just as thrilled to imagine it from these pages.

In my new novel, *Lux*, one character is a pilot for a small commuter airline, Cape Cod Air. Having read Wolfgang Langewiesche's manual, I could give more exact and lively description to my scenes inside the little Cessna nine-seater, and from these realist details characterization is strengthened. I could show "how" my pilot makes his climb, or tries "the Mushing Glide," so as not to overshoot a touchdown at a Logan runway. *Stick and Rudder* examines these flying gaits, describing "angle of attack," which is different from "angle of incidence," which is different from "attitude." "Attitude" being where the nose is pointed, and "angle of attack" is "how the wing meets the air."

Don't you know that!

My female character, later, in a bedroom scene, imagines some of this flight philosophy she'd heard about from the pilot, as she undresses. Suddenly all these evocative phrases from Langewiesche's *Stick and Rudder* begin to offer metaphoric prisms that can be exploded, cracked open like geodes in the pages of fiction.  ✧

# HEADLESS by Benjamin Weissman

Amy Gerstler

Hello, you who may be reading this while munching a pastrami on rye dripping with thousand island dressing. I too am a reading glutton. Like you, perhaps, I am almost always thinking about what I want to read, what I have read that was inspiring and/or puzzling, and what I am looking forward to rereading soon—much as someone obsessed with food ruminates about remembered delicacies already digested and those yet to be cooked and ecstatically consumed. And when I think about the book that whets my appetite most lately, I find myself compelled to make a curious admission. The book I am eagerly anticipating above all others at the moment is *Headless* by Benjamin Weissman, his second book of short stories, published in January and it happens that I am married to its author. It seems wrong not to admit my relationship to this writer up front. But it also seemed wrong to shy away from writing about *Headless* for that reason, because my admiration for this book is so profound that I am dead certain I would be crazy about it regardless of how I felt about the man who produced it. Bret Easton Ellis gave this book what I think is a very spot-on blurb: "Brilliant. Wildly inventive, profane, and hilarious. Benjamin Weissman is a master stylist who in story after story keeps scoring effortlessly. Beneath the deadpan absurdity these virtuoso comic monologues describe with more intense accuracy than just about anybody around what it means to be male." The stories in this book are dark, full of sex, violence, tenderness, comedy, and satire. They are smart and elegant as well as sometimes scatological, ringing with the voice of the eloquent, lyrical, manic id. Kafka, David Lynch, Melville, Hawthorne and Quentin Tarantino seem to be Benjamin's aesthetic kin. I think his writing also has links to the likes of George Saunders, Denis Johnson, and Rick Moody. He is a fan of Barthelme, John Hawkes, and Mary Gaitskill in case all this listing of names helps you situate yourself literarily here. He writes with scrupulous attention to the pleasure of sentences, to the extent that some of the shorter texts read like prose poems. The stories range from pieces proffering sexual advice from a variety of "expert" sources, a monologue about the tragic consequences of plumbing disasters, the predicament of a man invited by a female friend to impregnate her while he happens to be on his honeymoon, the cartoonish fairy tale of love between a lumberjack and short-order cook, a play in which a father is tormented by his insatiable consumer culture young sons, the confession of a man who has had intimate relations with a bear, and much more. This is a rich, strange, emotional book, the very last word of which, somewhat paradoxically, is "joy."

Other works I have been chewing on and finding tasty of late are: John D'Agata's anthology *The Next American Essay*, and Colson Whitehead's *The Colossus of New York*. In the history department I have been rereading Christopher Smart. And I have been saving up my allowance to buy Evan Connell's biography of Goya when it comes out. Bon appetit. ✧

# HEED THE THUNDER by Jim Thompson

Neal Pollack

**P**eople often ask me about my favorite novel, and I tell them about *Heed The Thunder*, both because it really is my favorite novel and because I'm almost certain that they've never read it or even looked at it twice at the bookstore. Readers know Thompson for his short, terse, funny crime novels, which really aren't crime novels at all, but they've been mischaracterized as such. Still there are crimes in most of the novels, the ones that aren't about building an oil pipeline in Texas or working in a San Diego shipyard. Damn, I love Jim Thompson.

*Heed The Thunder* is an entirely different animal. Early 1900s Nebraska, according to our educations, is Willa Cather territory. Well, Willa Cather never wrote a novel rife with incest, syphilis, and a hulking man-beast waiting to give an arrogant dandy his just desserts. But this book is also deeply knowing about politics and economics and agriculture. It understands the dynamics of a family at the end of its line. And in the end, it even manages to turn itself into a sentimental coming-of-age story. It is funny and rich and strange in a way that most contemporary novels can't approach.

If I had to teach one American novel, it would be *The Great Gatsby*. The second would be *The Day Of The Locusts*. *Heed The Thunder* would be third. In fact, I think I'm going to reread it right now. ✧

# LUCY GAYHEART by Willa Cather

Mary Morris

I came to Willa Cather late. It was odd that she escaped me because as a girl and young woman I read books that grew out of my love of the heartland where I am from. I read Twain, Dreiser, and, of course, Laura Ingalls Wilder, but never Cather. In a sense I believe that books come to us at the right time and that's how Willa Cather came to me. It wasn't until I was married and living in New Mexico that I read *Death Comes to the Archbishop*. I was mesmerized by the gift of her storytelling, the cumulative effect of the narrative delivered with grace and ostensible simplicity.

A few years later when I was teaching at Princeton, I started talking about Cather with a friend who said, "But you haven't read *My Antonia*?" It was her favorite book in the world and she told me how lucky I was—to read this book for the first time as a grown-up. I read it as one might listen to a person who is slowly coming to discover a life-long friend. Cather grew on me in that way, but it wasn't until I caught a small squib in the newspaper that my bond was truly, irrevocably, formed.

A newspaper account said that for years Joanne Woodward had been trying to make a film out of the Cather novella *Lucy Gayheart*. I'd never heard of *Lucy Gayheart*, but I went out and got it. I opened it and read these lines:

> In Haverford on the Platte, the townspeople still talk of Lucy Gayheart. They do not talk of her a great deal, to be sure; life goes on and we live in the present. But when they do mention her name it is with a gentle glow in the face or the voice, a confidential glance which says: "Yes, you, too, remember?"

I settled into my chair with a cup of tea and my dog at my side, because I knew that someone was going to tell me a story about a person's life filled with all the tenderness and nostalgia I felt for the Middle West and a childhood I too had left behind. From the moment I began *Lucy Gayheart*, which opens with a touching, but portentous skating scene and ends with one of the most poignant images in fiction, I knew I had come home.

I found myself for days, living in a parallel universe with Lucy and Harry and the town of Haverford, the corrupting Chicago. The heartbreak of disappointment and mistakes that cannot be made right. Then I read the other short Cather novellas—*A Lost Lady* and *Alexander's Bridge*. But *Lucy Gayheart* was the turning point for me. I had found my American Chekhov.

I realize I am not the first to feel this way about Willa Cather and I feel somewhat naive as if I am stating the obvious. But Cather came to me at a moment when I needed her. I had forgotten what it was that I loved about writing and being a writer. Why I'd begun this in the first place.

What has drawn me into Cather is the clarity of her uncluttered prose—as vast and lonely as the places she writes about. There are no pyrotechnics of language, no tap dancing turns of phrase. It is language stripped to its essentials; everything exists for the purpose of the story. When people speak of Hemingway and Raymond Carver in terms of clean, clear sentences devoted to the telling of the story I do not know why Cather is not mentioned in the same breath.

I have long been a fan of Midwestern Writers and intrigued by their migratory patterns and by the fact that from afar what they write about most is home. Fitzgerald, Hemingway, Dreiser, Twain, Nathaniel West, and, more recently, Baxter, Dybek, Patricia Hampl. Writers of straightforward, no-nonsense prose whose goal is to create characters we care about who live inside a story we want to hear. It is what writers are supposed to do.

We read these writers. And by that I mean we don't have to ponder them or explicate them or use the dictionary to understand them. We read them as if someone was stoking a fire or sitting on a front stoop and telling us something we had never heard before. We grow patient and the business of our lives comes to a halt as if we've got nothing but time and follow the story as if being led by the hand.

Alberto Moravio once said that life is chaos; only literature makes sense. It's as if someone has come in and straightened up the house. And for me that someone is Willa Cather. ✧

# Some Things About Kevin Brockmeier
Thisbe Nissen

### I.

Kevin Brockmeier is the author of a brilliant story collection, *Things That Fall From The Sky*; a heartbreakingly beautiful novel, *The Truth About Celia*; and a children's novel called *City of Names*.

### 2.

The first thing I ever read by Kevin Brockmeier was a story called "A Day in the Life of Half of Rumpelstiltskin," and I didn't get it. I remember telling people: "This guy in my grad program, I read a story he wrote—he's in workshop with a friend of mine—so in this story the main character is literally half of Rumpelstiltskin! You know how he gets split down the middle or something at the end of the fairy tale ...? So this story is half of him after the split—and he goes through all about how Rumpelstiltskin gets around, you know, hurtling his one leg out in front of him or something, and the two halves of Rumpelstiltskin write letters to each other in the form of Mad Libs ...? It's totally insane! I mean: this is what people are writing?" This was decidedly not what I had expected from graduate school. I was twenty-two and a moron; Kevin was, I think, twenty-three, and brilliant.

### 3.

The second thing I ever read by Kevin Brockmeier was "The Passenger," a story which takes place entirely aboard an airplane, because the world is an airplane: people are born with their luggage in the overhead compartment, stewardesses perform rites of passage, complimentary beverages are served. The narrator is in love with the woman in the seat in front of him, but he can't get up the nerve to talk to her. This story—which I read in the form of xeroxed computer printouts stapled together, its author's name in the upper left-hand corner, *Graduate Fiction Workshop* followed by the name of the professor, a date in early 1996—this story brought me to tears. Literal tears. Actual tears. It made me cry. I thought it was beautiful and heartbreaking and wondrous. I saw Kevin in the hall at school, introduced myself and gushed at him. His reaction seemed to be a mixture of honest humility, heartfelt gratitude and genuine surprise.

### 4.

We used to drive out to a lake near campus in the spring and summer to sing songs. He knows songs, Kevin Brockmeier, folk songs, tons of them. We'd sing together the ones we both knew and sing the others to each other, little solo performances, those songs we so desperately wanted each other to hear. He's got an amazing, amazing voice, Kevin does—rich and soulful—a voice you can hardly believe emanates from his body.

5.

No one has yet been able to satisfactorily disprove my contention that Kevin Brockmeier subsists solely on breakfast cereal (though Boo Berry didn't turn out to be as divine as he'd remembered it from a snowy morning in childhood), popsicles, and the occasional can of vegetarian soup. I know this. He had no car. I took him grocery shopping.

6.

Kevin Brockmeier owns so many books he used to have to stack them on the floor of his apartment because he couldn't fit any more bookshelves in the place. I think his apartment is a little bigger now. He needs to have enough free floor space because he likes to lie flat on the floor to think. He likes, if possible, for the floor to be carpeted. It's more comfortable that way.

7.

The day Kevin Brockmeier's story "These Hands" went up for workshop my best friend was visiting me and planned to sit in on the class. She's not a writer, and though she's an avid reader and an English teacher to boot she still tends to hold back her gut reactions to literature when in the presence of my writer-friends and me. She took Kevin's story into the other room to read it before class and crept out sometime later with a funny look on her face, wary of saying something that might offend my snobby writerly sensibilities, but so clearly moved by the story she had to say something. She spoke tentatively: "So this guy," she began, "he's a genius, right?" "Yes," I said. About that there was nothing to dispute. ✧

# THE LIFE TO COME AND OTHER STORIES by E. M. Forster
Christopher Castellani

Rarely do we get to peek into the pornography of great writers. Though we can speculate about what we might have found between the mattresses of the dead white males, few theories can be confirmed. Not so with E. M. Forster. In fact, many readers and admirers are not aware that Forster wrote his own pornography—a dozen or so short stories collected in the bawdy little volume, *The Life to Come*.

Forster wrote these stories "not to express myself but to excite myself" and knew they (like *Maurice*) dealt too candidly with sexuality to be published in his lifetime. Unlike *Maurice*, though, the stories are far from romantic or sentimental. They are brutal, eerie, ironic, damning of a hypocritical society, and more than a little twisted, even by today's standards—all without resorting to a single explicit sex scene. As in all great literature, the characters in *The Life to Come* are fully human and encounter various emotional obstacles; most of them just happen to involve illicit trysts.

Found among Forster's personal memoranda was this 1935 confession: "I want to love a strong young man of the lower classes and be loved by him and even hurt by him. That is my ticket, and then I have wanted to write respectable novels." Forster knew these two desires—to be loved and to be admired—could not peacefully coexist. So, in the forty-six years between his final novel, *A Passage to India*, and his death in 1970, he wrote and/or revised the stories in *The Life to Come* as well as a number of scholarly works. While the novels and essays are traditional in form and content, the stories embrace the fantastic and supernatural; a few may even be classified as historical or science fiction. Deliciously, they show a side of Forster you won't find in his "respectable" efforts.

For example: In "The Obelisk," a married couple out sightseeing are led separately into the bushes and seduced by two swarthy sailors; in another set of bushes, this time a prim English garden, an older gentleman has his way with young "Arthur Snatchfold," then betrays him; "The Other Boat," is the creepy tale of a murderous relationship between Lionel and Cocoanut ("Nordic warrior and subtle supple boy, who belonged to no race and always got what he wanted"); in the dark African forest of the title story, tribal chief Vithobai gives Paul Pinmay, a missionary, quite a dramatic send-off into the afterlife.

Forster's obsession with the power dynamics of interracial and intergenerational relationships, as well as relationships between people of different social classes, are on full display in *The Life to Come*. The obsession is easy to notice, but less easy to categorize, analyze or judge. The stories seem clearly about punishment and shame, guilt and revenge, but on closer examination, they resist easy answers, complicate expectations and provide a rich context for the novels, including *Maurice*. You'll never read (or watch) *A Room With a View* quite the same way again.

And yes, of course the title is a pun. These stories might be thought of as Forster's vision of the future, the lives that will be led by men other than him. Or we can take the author at his word, and think of these characters' experiences as merely his own sexual fantasies transmuted into literature. If there's a political message, it might simply be this: you've only got one life to find satisfaction; don't count on whatever's next.

Take poor Paul Pinmay, for example. "We have erred in this life," he tells his converted Vithobai as they embrace, "but it will not be so in the life to come." Moments later, Vithobai stabs him through the heart.  ✧

# Truman Capote, Richard Ford and John Irving

Lewis Robinson

### 1. *A Capote Reader*

When he wrote *In Cold Blood* (which is not included in this collection) it was clear that Truman Capote was answering a challenge. What's equally clear: he delivered. It's a virtuoso performance, a book about killers written, it seems, by one with fresh blood on his hands. *A Capote Reader* contains a different brand of work, writing that summons the melancholic, narcotic sensation of waking from deep sleep.

Capote often reminded interviewers that he was a genius—an obnoxious claim—but this collection offers no reason to refute it. Check out the wide-eyed travel sketches from the 40s, when he was new to the world as a writer: on New Orleans, on Haiti, on Tangier. Thirty years later, his essays "A Day's Work," "Self-Portrait," and "Nocturnal Turnings" display a similar exuberance—but a sadness has crept in, and the work is all the better for it. In the heart of the book: *Breakfast at Tiffany's*. A satisfying record of a remarkable literary life.

### 2. *Independence Day* by Richard Ford

Not exactly underappreciated—it won the Pulitzer Prize—but here's a book that tops the list of modern books I wish I'd written. From beginning to end, Ford allows you to cringe at the failures of his narrator while at the same time hoping the poor guy will fail. I like Frank Bascombe, but I'm also satisfied when he trips himself up. The wonder is that Ford can sustain this. Also: how does Ford know so much about the business of real estate? The prose is confident but not arrogant; every detail about the humming lights of suburbia works on me.

### 3. *The Water-Method Man* by John Irving

First, a disclaimer: I used to work for the author. One day in mid-October of my first year in his employ, about ten years ago, I was sitting at my desk in the upstairs of his house in Vermont, and my ass started to cramp up. I was hankering for some time off. I had a window at my desk, with a decent view of the woods, and I could tell, with the window closed, it was one of those ridiculously perfect fall days, the kind of day when, if you're frolicking outside, there's a Vivaldi symphony blaring in your brain. But I wasn't frolicking outside. I was sitting at a desk with a sore ass. So I padded down to his office and crept up behind him. "Hey," I whispered. "It's National Secretary's Day." (It really was.) He didn't seem to get it.

"*I'm your secretary,*" I said.

"No," he said. "You're not. You're my *assistant.*"

He continued typing. I returned to my desk.

We had a good rapport. But that afternoon, it was early enough in my tenure that I hadn't yet learned how to interpret his manner. Was he being funny? Was he being semantically particular? Was he being grumpy? The answer (and I'm sure of it, now) is that he wanted to joust. In my time working for him, he was good at this. Yes, he could wield a mighty joust—with playful intent, always—and these joustings came to be the main entertainment of the job. We weren't competitive with each other, per se, but we did a fine job of giving at least some of our daily work a competitive spin. Whenever I gave him proofreading notes in response to new first-draft material, he'd hand back his arbitration of my comments in the form of a scorecard. "Five out of seven, today," he'd write. "Not bad." (Oh, and for the record: it turned out he always needed to be reminded of holidays, and not just the flimsy ones, like National Secretary's Day. If he wasn't tapped on the shoulder before, say, Thanksgiving, there was a good chance he'd pound on his typewriter clear through the weekend. Unlike me, he was never one to hanker for time off.)

I've met fans of Irving's work who dismiss the novels he wrote before *Garp* as less accomplished, less ambitious than the ones that came after. I have to admit I'm an admirer of all his books, but my special affection for *The Water-Method Man* comes from its unbridled mania. This book could fuel an aircraft carrier. Take Irving's intensity, his muscularity, his ability to manage an epic narrative, and bring it to the loosy-goosey, free-love canvas of the early 1970s. What does a writer with a joust—a member of the National Wrestling Hall of Fame—do with a hippie commune, obscure graduate studies, and low-budget experimental filmmaking? He pins this stuff to the ground and tickles it. Irving brings us Fred "Bogus" Trumper, a grad-student intent on deciphering an indecipherable language, Old Low Norse, whose life is the subject of a documentary entitled *Fucking Up*. It's sterling satire, but, as in Irving's later work, the joust is brandished compassionately. ✧

# STONES FOR IBARRA by Harriet Doerr and OF KINKAJOUS, CAPYBARAS, HORNED BEETLES, SELEDANGS, AND THE ODDEST AND MOST WONDERFUL MAMMALS, INSECTS, BIRDS, AND PLANTS OF OUR WORLD by Jeanne K. Hanson and Deane Morrison

Gwendolen Gross

These two books do not go together. But of course, in some ways, they do. I've always been fond of odd associations: when I lived in San Francisco, my neighbors on hilly Valley Street constructed wild winter wonderland displays amidst their cacti-strewn, no-water landscaping, precipitous chunk of yard.

But these books are my neighbors as well; they sit on my shelves along with whatever else I haven't given away or relegated to the basement where there's space and cool, even in the summer.

I was lucky enough to meet Harriet Doerr at her Pasadena home, where, mostly blind, she gave me a tour of her garden and talked about writing characters. In the way she talked about both flowers and people, she revealed an exquisite way of seeing, the kind of vision—the eye—poets strive for, a kind of synesthesia of the known and the invented, of sensory reality and association. *Stones for Ibarra*, Doerr's first novel, describes another kind of vision: the vision afforded by distance. The just-over and just-under forty couple who unfold themselves for the lens of her book are Americans who move to a small village in Mexico to reopen a copper mine. Doerr manages to pull off these second and third sentences, "The driver of the station wagon is Richard Everton, a blue-eyed, black-haired stubborn man who will die thirty years sooner than he now imagines. On the seat beside him is his wife, Sara, who imagines neither his death nor her own, imminent or remote as they may be." We care about them, through the course of her book, the way we care for all mortals we know and believe and eat and talk with, even learning their mistakes and the other perspectives around them, even knowing about the death she has allowed us to foresee. *Consider This, Senora*, her second novel, is richly peopled as well; perhaps it's an easier read, but no less passionate, no less worth the journey.

*Of Kinkajous, Capybaras, Horned Beetles, Seledangs, and the Oddest and Most Wonderful Mammals, Insects, Birds, and Plants of Our World* by Jeanne K. Hanson and Deane Morrison may not live up to the length and superlatives of its title, but it's as refreshing as a walk through a please-touch science museum. I open it when I'm thinking we humans have far too complicated brains. Of course we do! Our companions in evolutionary splendor include orchids that mimic the shape or smell of female insects so the males of the insects' species will try to mate with them and in the process, pollinate. The word "orchid," Hanson and Morrison tell us, comes from the Greek word for testicle. A clown fish, explains a section called "Sex Changes in the Wild," changes from male to female when his mate dies. The book's organized into vignettes; there's nothing encyclopedic about it, except if you like to open encyclopedias (okay, I do) for brief hits of information. Not enough to write a thesis, just enough to start making all kinds of analogies. A small museum of wonders on the premises.

I think of San Francisco, and I think of winter, of gnomes, sleighs, fake snow, blooming ice plant, cacti, the works. When I sat down to write this I thought: what can I recommend that hasn't already graced a hundred Staff Recommendation tables? Those you know about already, but still, when I started a list, it was quickly longer than the word limit by itself. So I picked just two books, one emotionally profound, the other a reflection of our factually tantalized tastes, but both well worth a read.  ✧

# Words—Lean, Lyrical, Authentic—Bring Children From Shadows

Rachel Solar-Tuttle

This is the summer of children. In my mind's eye, I see them all the time. Children walking with backpacks on dusty roads. Hitching rides. A young man alone on a mailbox watching the world. Tiny bundles handed to social workers, their birth mothers in tears. Children fiercely playing grown-up, and only because they have to. Children on their way somewhere. Lost children. Found children.

Maybe children are on my mind because this is the summer our own child will arrive from the arms of his loving foster mother in Korea. She will have carried him on her back everywhere she went, wrapped in a podaegi, their breaths falling into the same warm rhythm. She will have beamed when the adoption agency workers complimented her on how well he was growing—look at those cheeks!—under her care.

The foster care stories I read this summer are stories from somewhere else, the other end of the world, where the word "care" hardly applies and any hope of comfort is jettisoned like the finest paper in the whipping winds of abuse and neglect.

Two lost children forced to grow up fast. Two haunting, first-person narratives. One a true story, one lyrical—but achingly authentic—fiction.

> Annmarie, my mother, had lied about who my father was, like she'd lied about so many other things in my life before the night she drove me in the pitch dark to grandma's, leaving me half-asleep for grandma to find with the milk and the morning paper.

So begins the path of Miriam, the bright, wry, courageous protagonist who springs to life at the deft hands of Lisa Borders in *Cloud Cuckoo Land* (River City Publishing, 2002). If only Miri could have stayed with her grandmother in Prairie Rose, Texas. Instead, when her grandmother dies, she starts along a pathway that carries her from state to state, from foster home to foster home, and eventually to the streets, her grit and golden voice her only protection.

Borders expertly spins a story about survival, music, love, loss, and the meaning of family. Miri is one of those characters who is so well realized that she transcends the realm of "character," leaping off the page and grabbing the reader's hand, a true and painfully lovable person who makes every turn of the narrative resonate and leaves the reader wondering about the others, the children who slip into the dark fissures of the foster care system and live in the shadows of every city.

Antwone Fisher really is one of those others, and his autobiography *Finding Fish* (Perennial, 2001) gives voice to lost children everywhere, a laid bare, honest voice that stays with me in dreams. The autobiography differs vastly from *The Antwone Fisher Story*, the Denzel Washington film of earlier this year. *Finding Fish* spends the bulk of its time not on Fisher's years in the Navy, but on his years of treachery in the non-home of the Pickett family, a foster situation in which he is physically, psychologically, and/or sexually abused on a daily basis.

Within this utterly unsentimental telling of some of the most despicable acts imaginable against a child, one of the most affecting ways that Fisher brings the reader into his world is not through the descriptions of abuse, but through the long and loving attention he gives to the crumbs of pleasure he cobbles together growing up: a kind teacher who lets him clap erasers after school, a moment listening to a song by the Dramatics, daydreaming at a window, sitting on a mailbox and watching the world go by, a compliment, the joy he takes in cleaning a room or creating a window display in his tormentor's second-hand store.

It is the lingering attention Fisher pours on these slivers of happiness that enables us to peek into the horrors of his experience, the terror that makes the kind of small moments most of us disregard the lynchpins of Fisher's survival.

As Miri has her music, Fisher has his imagination, and later, his ability to write. The autobiography is peppered with Fisher's poetry, which gives stops for breathing amidst the heartbreak and offers reminders of the man that he—through an unflappable inner strength cultivated with so little outside nourishment—ultimately becomes. In one of these poems, he asks, "Who will cry for the little boy?/A good boy he tried to be. Who will cry for the little boy./Who cries inside of me?" In telling his story, he ensures that we do cry—not only for this little boy, but for those others who do not make it.

When my husband and I fill out our adoption papers, one of our tasks is to write a pledge to the other children, "the children left behind" in Korea. What will we do to see that they are cared for, that we do not just take our son and walk away from the bigger picture? *Finding Fish* and *Cloud Cuckoo Land* are survival stories of left-behind children who find their way. But the story that they tell between the lines is perhaps most haunting of all, the story of those who stay lost. I write my pledge letter with wet eyes, folding the stories of Miri and Antwone into that envelope. I send it across the ocean, dreaming shadowy dreams of children.  ✧

# STORIES IN THE WORST WAY by Gary Lutz

David Ryan

Knopf's original hardback cover of Gary Lutz's debut collection, *Stories in the Worst Way*—reprinted last year by *3rd bed*—displayed three small Chinese condiment containers raised in fantastically plastic, shiny relief. What was inside the book is less describable

Like the title, and that edition's cover, Gary Lutz's stories hinge the commonplace onto itself, skewing the environment just enough to create a kind of unnerving fission between the familiar and some other dimension that isn't quite its doppelganger: like waking up from a dream in which you were dreaming you were sleeping. It is this transmission—the common life bent just so, that it doesn't feel comfortable in the space it's been attributed—that makes his work so perplexing and simultaneously joyful to read. He refuses to write a sentence anyone has heard, read, or even thought before. I suspect it is this strangeness, this responsibility foisted onto the listener/reader/thinker that makes Lutz less known than, say, Richard Ford. And then the psychology of his stories—in which obsessive, dislocated characters often search for emotional life's tangibility, relevancy, but eventually give up their search and simply catalog the contents of bathroom trash, or the receding quality of their own failing gumline—is too close for some. You have to labor with the writing because the writer refuses to put anything in quite its familiar context. It is only after you penetrate the unfamiliarity that it becomes suddenly too familiar, and kind of scary in its reality.

The irony is that there is a great generosity in Lutz's dialect, his ability to change language, to make it different than everything else; his characters, and readers, are beholden to it alone. Words drive any human tendency here, their anthropomorphosis as complex and conflicted and complete as the math inside a human cell or smear of DNA. Words gather to take on a shape in his fictions, they presume their characters' wills, grow their own appendages, breathe, worry, wander off and then maybe the story ends, maybe it just hangs in the air. If Lutz's phrasing and syntax are detached from convention, his characters, floating about, are often even lonelier.

But what people most often hesitate to see is how funny this guy is. You sometimes laugh immediately, often a few hours later, once the joke finally registers, and sometimes not at all, as you're suddenly too preoccupied with the prettiest/ugliest thing you've ever read. Other times the comic effect is that of pure rhetorical magic: no need to laugh, there is equally joyful recognition in the juxtaposition he's pulling off. If timing is everything in comedy, ultimately what may divide Lutz's readership, is that even this—the timing of his humor—is as arresting and original as the prose. He writes anti-comedies, and in this way I'd argue he most closely descends from Beckett, or Kafka, of any writer I've read.

I realized last night reading again from the new collection, *I Looked Alive* (which should be available from Black Square Editions by the time you read this), just how well he's extended the word into an even more mature, funny, and disarming realm than his already auspicious *Stories in the Worst Way*. This is a writer who deserves ranking among the great stylists, and who—like many of them—may suffer the common fate of not being appreciated, initially, beyond the poor will of convention, of a so-called "difficulty." When all along he's simply writing the future. Neglect would be a shame—for his living talent, but more so for the reader. ✧

# MORVERN CALLAR by Alan Warner

Jaime Clarke

That this book is almost ten years old now comes as a bit of a shock to me, such is its imprint in my mind—both as a reader and as a writer. Every writer (and every reader, too) marks his or her understanding of fiction with those touchstone texts that moves us along, gently (but sometimes violently) uprooting us so that we look in the rearview mirror with wonder, chuckling at what we thought we once knew.

For me, *Morvern Callar* is one of those sacred books. I owe its discovery to one of my former writing teachers, Amy Hempel, whose personal reading list was something of a wake-up call (and a stated challenge) in graduate school, especially for someone who professes a love for so-called voice fiction, which I did (and do).

That true literary fiction should be character-driven (versus the plot mechanisms of popular fiction) is a widely regarded and generally-accepted definition among practitioners of the art; however, it is still unusual, and cause for celebration, when an author successfully creates a wholly original character, as Warner does with the title character in this ingenious book.

Coming home from her dissatisfying job at the local supermarket in a port town in western Scotland, Morvern Callar finds that her boyfriend has committed suicide on the kitchen floor by slitting his throat. A suicide note instructs her to send his manuscript out to publishers on his behalf. After the shock wears off, Morvern makes two shocking decisions that fuel the narrative. First, she chops up her dead boyfriend and stores him in the attic. Next, she does indeed solicit publishers on behalf of the finished manuscript in her possession—with one small change: she erases her boyfriend's name and inserts her own. An advance sent by a London publisher is the get-out-of-jail-free card Morvern has always dreamed of and, grabbing up her best friend, Lanna, they make for the Spanish coast in a blur of raves, drugs, and pop music, with some surprise plot points along the way.

The story of *Morvern Callar*, however, is not the what, when, where and how, but the who. The demands on voice fiction are multiple: the narration is more oftentimes than not first-person, a device that requires caution on the writer's part and patience on the part of the reader; the first-person narration striving for originality will likely invent or incorporate several colloquial elements to forge a vernacular, a risk that either pays off in spades or obliterates the reader's interest on the first page; and finally, voice fiction shares with its third- (and sometimes second-) person brethren the desire to have the reader understand the narrator more deeply than the narrator understands him or herself, all of which is quite a balancing act, one that Warner manages deftly. What offsets contrived or familiar (or convenient) plot elements is the hypnotic nature of Movernspeak, an admixture of pop cultural slang, Scottish colloquy, and a surface cool that is alternately exhilarating and chilling. And Morvern's propensity for nicknames is nothing short of hilarious. Too, the sometimes-awkward-but-mostly brilliant sentence constructions (created sometimes by dropping articles, or shuffling phrases around Latinate-style) lend the novel a verve that can only be credited to the author's brilliant powers.

Sample the novel's opening paragraphs:

He'd cut His throat with the knife. He'd near chopped off His hand with the meat cleaver. He couldn't object so I lit a Silk Cut. A sort of wave of something was going across me. There was a fright but I'd daydreamed how I'd be.

He was bare and dead face-down on the scullery lino with blood round. The Christmas tree lights were on then off. You could change the speed those ones flashed at. Over and over you saw Him stretched out then the pitch dark with His computer screen still on.

I started the greeting on account of all the presents under our tree and Him dead. Useless little presents always made me sad.

Read on for an unbelievable ride through a foreign landscape with an unforgettable guide you're not likely to encounter again, either in your real-world travels or in your pursuits across the landscape of fiction. ✧

# ETCETERA

## POST ROAD

# nebraska summer writers' conference

## JUNE 19–25, 2004

Join award-winning writers from around the country for workshops and panels in the novel, short story, poetry, travel & nature writing, mystery, memoir, screen-writing, and publishing. Have your writing assessed by a New York publisher and literary agents.

weekend and week-long workshops

For more information visit the web site

## http://www.nswc.org

or contact **Jonis Agee,** conference director at 402.472.1834 *or* nswc@unl.edu *or* jagee@unl.edu

University of Nebraska / Lincoln NE

RITA MAE BROWN

CARL PHILLIPS

ROBERT OLEN BUTLER

PAM HOUSTON

MARY PIPHER

JANE BARNES

HILDA RAZ

ELIZABETH DEWBERRY

SHARON OARD WARNER

GRACE BAUER

MARCOS VILLATORO

AGENTS EMMA SWEENEY & WENDY WEIL

PENGUIN PUBLISHER JANE VON MEHREN

& OTHERS

Nebraska
UNIVERSITY OF
Lincoln

# Warnings

Amy Kreines

**Warning: hazardous material.**
This drug may impair the ability to drive or operate machinery. This drug may cause hair loss. Warning: use of this drug may cause drowsiness or sexual side-effects. Consumption of alcohol while using this drug may cause serious health risks. Do not use when pregnant. Warning: contains Phenylalanine. Warning: consult doctor before use. Hazardous to health. May cause internal bleeding. May cause loss of vision. May cause death.

**Warning: keep in a secure location.**
Keep away from open flame. Do not stare directly into the flame. Do not ignite: may cause explosion. Keep away from face. Keep away from children. Keep out of reach of children. Children under two are at risk when using this product. This package is for households without young children. If safety seal is tampered with, do not use product.

**Do not use product before reading instructions.**
Do not use this product if cap has been tampered with. Do not use this product if label is torn. Do not use this product if safety seal has been popped. Do not enter. Do not use stairs. Do not use this door. Do not open this door. Do not open window. Warning: window does not open. Do not use this exit. Do not turn light off. Do not touch light switch. Do not open the fuse box. Warning: contains electrical material. Warning: danger of electric shock. Warning: static electricity. Do not place near water when in use. Do not immerse in water. Do not use if you have a history of heart problems. Do not use unless room is well-ventilated. Do not use if you are ill, or have recently been ill. Do not use excessively. Please use product liberally. Do not place in extreme cold. Keep in a cool, dry place.

**Warning: may cause confusion.**  ✧

# Joseph Brodsky
Sven Birkerts

I knew Joseph Brodsky, not well by some standards, but with such exaggerated eagerness on my part that his influence remains, even now, eight years after his death, enormous. I don't mean his literary influence—though his effect there was considerable—but what might be called his tutelary presence. The man had an intensity such as I'd never encountered before. Nor have I since. In his presence literature and writing finally mattered as I knew they should, and this mattering redeemed all the slights and rudenesses that he inflicted as he made his way through our midst. I know that there are many who won't grant that absolution, but they also very likely missed out on the full force of his personality.

In 1973, when Brodsky came to live in Ann Arbor, Michigan, I was in my last year at the University of Michigan. He was a major news item before he even arrived, a dissident hero. This was the young poet who had stood up to the Soviet State, proclaiming the sovereign right of the poet to speak his vision, and winning the adoration of literati the world over. Released from a sentence of hard labor (a concession to pressure from international writers and intellectuals), freed to emigrate to Israel, Brodsky changed his itinerary when he got to Vienna. He ended up accepting an offer extended by Carl Proffer, a professor and editor of the journal Ardis, to come to Michigan as poet-in-residence.

Brodsky's first public reading was a very big event in the Ann Arbor community. My girlfriend and I, I remember, felt lucky to have gotten our seats at the far rear of Rackham Auditorium. The poet was much introduced and much applauded. Ann Arbor's own poetic eminence, Donald Hall, was up on stage to offer the translations. And when Brodsky finally took the lectern and declaimed—he consulted no text—the effect was electrifying. Since, of course, it has become part of Brodsky lore—the incantatory magic of his Russian "performances"—but then it was new to all of us. The young poet with the long red hair and tragic features—a sharply beaked nose, a wide, downwardly-grimacing mouth—sang out his lines in a keening fury that brought down the house.

In the five or six years Brodsky spent in Ann Arbor, he never succumbed to the relentless community domestication, generally achieved there, as everywhere, through departmental interactions and punishing rounds of social activity; he never lost his fierce exoticism. He was not a local force, to be comprehended in the usual terms, but an international force. He flew to New York and London on weekends. He would be spotted in some local bar with his friend Mikhail Baryshnikov or the poet Anthony Hecht or some stunning woman said to be an Italian actress or a distant relation of Count Leo Tolstoy. He was known to be a ladies' man.

As for his teaching, those who knew said that his classes were impenetrable, not least because his English in those first months was a language adjacent to the one the rest of us spoke. Moreover, word was out that he suffered fools not at all.

When I left town in 1975 I had not yet read Brodsky's poems (his first English collection had recently been published). When I returned two years later, deeply depressed over a failed relationship, I knew the work cold. The poet's suffering was the only balm I could find that season, and when I saw him coming toward me on the street or buying a newspaper at the bookstore I was working in, I felt we had to become friends.

Once, overheated with lonely admiration—desperation—I put a note under his office door, praising his work and alluding to my own suffering, suggesting that if he wanted to get a drink sometime he should stop by the bookstore. He appeared the very next day, but when I saw him waiting by the counter I was seized with fear and could not get myself to come down from the mezzanine to introduce myself.

When I did, a few months later, finally speak to Brodsky, it was in that very same spot in the bookstore. Only now I was working across the street, managing a used and rare bookshop. I had come into Borders for a Sunday paper when I saw the poet standing by the register, gesticulating, trying to explain something to the clerk. I listened in and thought I understood. He was looking for *The Education of Henry Adams*, which was out of print. I knew that we had copy on the shelves in the other store and, butting into their stalled exchange, I indicated that he should follow me. The gods were on my side. I got him the book and we began—haltingly—to talk. I ended up inviting him to have coffee in my apartment just down the street. There the two of us chain-smoked and played the "have you read?" game for longer than seemed possible. He trumped me at every turn, of course, and I worried he would think me ignorant. But he seemed happy enough to be with someone who even recognized the names of writers like Milosz, Pavese, Mandelstam, and Tsvetaeva.

At this time, back in the mid-1970s, Brodsky still had the air of an enfant terrible. Impatient, aggressive, chain-smoking cigarettes, he liked creating dispute for its own sake. Suggest white and he would insist black. Admit an admiration—unless it was for one of his idols—like Auden or Lowell or Milosz—and he would overturn the opinion. "Minor," he would say of some eminence I mentioned. Or: "The man is an idiot." At first I did not understand the workings of this compulsion, and as we talked, drinking cup after cup of black coffee, I grew despondent. Here was my chance to meet the poet I had admired for so long, and I could say nothing right. Yet for all that, he seemed in no hurry to leave.

I would like to say that by the end of that long afternoon we had become friends, intimates, but that would not be true. I was, I think, too young and callow; I did not offer enough ground for real exchange. Instead, Brodsky assumed a fond, almost paternal role with me, teasing, chiding, offering suggestions about books. A limit was set. I did not feel that I was getting close to the turbulent soul that wrote the poems.

From that time on, though, we did stay in contact. Brodsky would suddenly show up in the bookstore, searching for some book of poems. On several occasions, too, he handed me the typescript of some essay he was working on for the *New York Review of Books*, asking if I would check over his English. The task would invariably keep me at my desk for hours, for the fact is that brilliant and inflammatory as his insights were, the prose at this stage was a bramble patch—English deployed as if it were an inflected language.

Once, I remember, I stayed up much of the night, recasting sentence by sentence his discussion of the Greek poet Cavafy, finally typing the whole thing over afresh. When I handed the piece to him the next day, he quickly glanced down the page, smiled his wicked sultan smile, and put the whole bundle in an envelope to mail. I never found out what he thought of my deeply deliberated interventions.

At the end of the summer—1976—I asked Brodsky if I could audit his modern poetry seminar in the fall. He greeted my question with a conspiratorial laugh, as if by letting me attend he was putting something over on the system. And so, come September, I left my bookstore perch two afternoons a week, crossing campus to a sterile brick building where I joined a small group of nervous others around an enormous conference table.

If we were nervous, it was because our instructor made us so. Whatever extracurricular connection I had with Brodsky counted for nothing at all. There was only the poem and the dynamics of the encounter.

Brodsky was at one and the same time the worst and the most vital and compelling teacher I've ever had. Worst because he did nothing, absolutely nothing, to make our confrontation with a difficult body of poetry pleasant or conventionally instructive. In part this was owing to his inexperience—he had never taught before coming to Ann Arbor—and in part to the fact that his English was even yet a work in progress. But mainly it was an expression of who he was and what he believed about poetry. Poetry was not something to be "gotten," mastered and regurgitated in paraphrase. It was not some thing one notched on the belt of attainments. It was, rather, a struggle waged in fear and trembling, an encounter with the very stuff of language that might put our core assumptions about existence into jeopardy. Brodsky would bring his students—us—into the arena, but he would not fight our battles for us. It could feel almost sadistic. All of us, at times, felt utterly exposed, not only in our ignorance, or the blandness of our assumptions about poetry, but in our way of reading the world.

"What do you think of this one?" he might begin, pointing to some poem we were to have read by Mandelstam, or Akhmatova, or Montale . . . Brodsky's tone on these occasions carried—I don't think I imagined this—a slightly bored, contemptuous edge, but also, to quote Auden (his favorite) quoting Serge Diaghilev, a sense of "astonish me." He made each of us want to say the brilliant thing, to earn that rarest of accolades: "Terrific!" But anxiety was usually more powerful. The question would be posed and the room would grow silent—a deep, sedimentary silence.

Somehow we all pushed on, even managed to forge a certain prison-cell camaraderie—one that, oddly, included Brodsky himself. Which is not to say that he relaxed one bit his vigilance, his insistence on adequate response to what we were reading. But he somehow, bored sighs notwithstanding, made himself a part of our collective grappling inadequacy. How did he manage it?

Class after class, Brodsky would arrive in the room late, after we had all begun to fidget. He would be fingering an unlit cigarette, conveying thereby that he would much rather be alone somewhere, smoking it, than in our midst. And then, almost invariably, he would heave up from his depths a shuddering, groaning sigh. But there was humor in it. For a moment later his beaked tragedy-mask expression would loosen. He would look slowly around the room and, taking us all in, smile, as though to communicate that at some level he knew what it must be like for us, as though to forgive us for our blandness.

But then it would start again, the relentless kneading of the language. A line from Mandelstam, a question, silence. Only when that silence had become unendurable would he lead us into the thickets of sound and association, with asides on the logic of poetic images, abbreviated lessons on the ethics of utterance, on the metaphysics of nouns, of rhymes . . .

Time passed. I left Ann Arbor and moved to Boston to seek my way as a writer. Brodsky moved to New York, which would remain his center of operations for the rest of his life. Once every few months I would screw up my courage and call his number. Our phone conversations were difficult, at least from my side. I always felt flat, uninteresting. I had no gossip to retail, did not move in those circles; I had no strident views to advance. I had begun writing essays on my own but I did not dare to inflict them on him. My best bet, I knew, was to offer praise. So I usually waited to make my calls until Brodsky had published some new essay or poem. Leading with a compliment seemed to work. Nor was Brodsky the kind to rebuff any kind words. "Ya," he would say, laughing, "it was pretty good, I must say." In person, his response to praise would be to put his hands together like paws and make a happy panting sound.

I don't know exactly when Brodsky began to suffer heart problems, but I do remember, in the late 1970s, there were long spells of worry among his friends. Word was that he'd had a heart attack, major by-pass surgery. I didn't get many of the details. I only knew that calling had become even more difficult, for now there was every chance that he would be in one of his dark moods. No conversational gambit worked then, not even praise. Offer up some compliment and he would often sigh impatiently and mutter something like, "It doesn't matter in the slightest." Whereupon long silence would follow. Brodsky, neither then nor ever, felt any responsibility for the niceties. If dead air was what was available, then dead air it would be.

In 1979, I proposed to interview Brodsky for *The Paris Review*, and got his permission. This was a very big thing for me. I re-read all of the poems and the many essays I had saved from the pages of the *New York Review of Books*, and then, armed with a tape-recorder and a pile of blank cassettes, I got on the train for New York.

Brodsky let me into his Morton Street apartment—it was my first visit—and proceeded to field a series of telephone calls, some of them international, I noted. I was free to pace around, study his bookshelves, glance at the photographs displayed everywhere on the walls and mantle. On the way to the bathroom, I noted an exercise bike that seemed to be doing duty as a clothes-hanging device.

Finally Brodsky was off the phone and ready to give me his full attention. We sat down in his living room, facing each other across a low coffee table, and I turned the tape-recorder on. As always, Brodsky smoked furiously, every so often ripping the filter off his cigarette, the better to get at the tobacco. He answered my questions seriously, professionally; he was able to set aside the darker joking tonality of our usual interchanges. We sat for at least two hours, talking about his Leningrad childhood, his literary influences, various cities, admired writers. At some point we switched from coffee to beer, and I could feel both of us relaxing perceptibly.

During those two hours I felt that I got a kind of sidelong glimpse of Brodsky's New York life. The phone calls—he took them, but kept them short, announcing, when he hung up, "That was Mark Strand," and "That was Bob Silvers." He liked it that I was impressed. At other points various neighbors made themselves known, calling in to him as they crossed the back courtyard, or even just knocking and walking right in, as his close friend and upstairs neighbor Masha did.

I felt caught up in a wonderful turbulence, the literary life as I'd always imagined it might be lived. There was a typewriter, an old manual, serving as a kind of paperweight on a desk brimming with page-proofs. "I've missed every conceivable deadline," said Brodsky. Stacks and stacks of review copies were piled up near the front door. At the center of all this chaos, looking by turns agitated, sorrowful and wryly cunning—his expressions shifting with each new question—sat the poet. I felt so monochromatic beside him, so unevolved.

Every five minutes or so, whether he was finished with it or not, Brodsky flung another lit cigarette into the enormous fireplace at his side. I could see that the casualness of the action gave him satisfaction.

"I would like to die in Venice," he said at one point near the end of our conversation. More and more, I'd noticed, he came around to last things. Or, to pull a Brodskean inversion, first things. "There is only one subject that matters to me," he said, a few minutes later, "and that is time and what it does to a man."

I saw Brodsky on a number of occasions after that interview, but never in quite so sustained or focused a way.

Once, I remember, I was in New York for some reason and we were having a cup of coffee in a cafeteria. Brodsky watched with rapt expression as a fat young waitress leaned into an enormous wall refrigerator, finally emerging with a piece on pie on a plate. He turned to me, as serious as I have ever seen him, and observed: "Once you see something like that there is simply no point in going on." More than anything, I think, Brodsky loved these mergings of the banal and the metaphysical. They were the stuff of his most inspired improvisations, and when he struck off what he believed was "a good one" he would laugh with unaffectedly boyish glee.

A few years later—we had not seen each other for at least a year—I was at some reception and saw Brodsky coming toward me across the room. I smiled and stepped forward to say hello. Scarcely cracking a smile, he reached into my shirt pocket, extracted a cigarette, ripped off the filter, and walked away. "Kisses," he called over his shoulder. That was that.

Dozens of little encounters and little stories, but they all add up to the same thing. Brodsky, now a Nobel Prize winner, was getting very famous and very busy. He was also, steadily, losing his health. Others who knew him in these years have admitted the same thing. That the man emanated such energy and contrary aliveness that it was very hard to think of him as having a weak heart.

Still, I remember how for a long time I used to torment myself with the thought that one day the phone would ring and it would be someone telling me that Brodsky—Joseph—had died.

Which is very nearly what happened. My wife and I had gone out for dinner, leaving our children with their babysitter. When we got home, among the evening's many incidentals, as reported by our seven-year-old daughter, was the message that a friend had called to say something about someone named Joseph.

"How did he sound?"

"Kind of serious," she said.

And that was it. I called my friend and confirmed what I feared. Brodsky had died of a massive heart attack—at home in New York, not in Venice as he had once wished (though he is now buried in Venice). Then I lay in bed for a long time trying to find ways to think about this new fact. Hardest was the idea of absence—that a soul so crowded and intent could be taken away. All that knowing and supposing and seeing of things. Logically, I thought, this should leave more room for the rest of us. But I knew, sure as I ever knew anything, that the opposite was true. ✧

# INDEX:
# THE GREAT GATSBY by F. Scott Fitzgerald

Tom Murphy

Pagination follows the paperback edition of *The Great Gatsby* (The Authorized Text). New York: Collier/Macmillan, 1992. Subentries are sorted by first appearance of page number, with a few obvious exceptions.

"Blessed are the dead," 183
"Bles-sed pre-cious," 123
blind
   Wilson's garage a, 29
   dog's eyes, 41
   was drawn, 152
blinding signs, 85
blindness, eternal, of Eckleburg,
Doctor T. J., 28
bloomed, 22
blue
   eyes of Eckleburg, Doctor T. J., 27
   Wilson's eyes, 29
   Myrtle's dress, 30
   of the Mediterranean, 38
   Gatsby's gardens, 43
   chauffeur's uniform, 45
   paint, streak of hair like, 90
   Indian, monograms, 98
   nose of producer, 111
   sky, 124
   coupé, 132, 148
   leaves, 159
   quickening by the window, a, 167
   smoke of brittle leaves, 185
   lawn, 189
"boarder", the; See Klipspringer
boat, 124
Bois de Boulogne, 70
bond business, bonds, 7, 14, 46, 87-88, 174
books
   volumes on banking and credit
      and investment securities, 8
   "Simon Called Peter," 33, 34
   Clay's "Economics," 89
bootlegger, 65, 103, 114, 141; SeeGatsby,
Jay, rumors about
bores, 5
botanical references. See tree; flower,
  garden, green
   character names; See Daisy,
      Myrtle, Orchid, Lilly,
   ivy, vines, 9, 11, 149
botanical references *continued*

leaf, leaves, 22, 159, 161, 185
wheat, 27
oranges and lemons, 43
blooms, a hearse heaped with, 73
grass, 83, 87, 89, 169-70
jonquil, hawthorn, plum blossoms,
   kiss-me-at-the-gate, 96
apple green, 98
orchid, orchids, 111, 158, 159
blossomed like a flower, 117
overripe, funny fruits of New York, 132
windows bloomed with light, 149
shrubbery, 150
holly, 184
boy, boys, 163, 168, 171, 175, 188
brake, brakes, 64, 151; See accident; car
breast
   Jordan as small-breasted, 15
   pap of life, 117
   Daisy's bosom, 122
   Myrtle's left, 145
   of the new world, green, 189
Broadway, 33, 77
brown
   Myrtle's muslin dress, 31
   tint of Jordan's face, 185
Buccleuch, Dukes of, 7
Buchanan, Daisy
   Nick's second cousin once removed, 10
   her heart, 10, 19
   her laugh, 13; See voice
   her child, 14, 21, 82, 123-24
   reacts to Gatsby's name, 15, 82-83
   complains about her finger, 16
   tells of her child's birth, 21-22
   not a Catholic, 38
   her name shouted by Myrtle, 41
   furious about not hearing from
     Nick, 78
   her house in Louisville, 79
   wild rumors about, 80
   marriage to Tom, 80-81; See wedding
   doesn't drink, 82; See drunk
Buchanan, Daisy *continued*

driving
Owl-eyes on, 59
Jordan's philosophy of, 63, 186
Daisy was, 151
drug store, 34, 95, 115, 127, 141
drunk
Nick, just twice in his life, 33
Nick on his way to get, 46
Owl-eyes, in library, 49-50
driver of shorn-wheel accident, 59
Snell, on the gravel drive, 66
Daisy, before wedding, 81
Dan Cody, 106
Miss Baedeker, 112-13
Catherine, after Myrtle's accident, 164
woman in a white evening dress, 185
Duluth, 106
dusk; See twilight
a pleasant street at, 18
velvet, 21
young clerks in, 62
Myrtle rushed out into, 144
Dutch sailors, 189; See exploration

## E

Earl of Doncaster, 71
east [direction]; See west
Europe, in relation to America, 7,
49; See exploration
Long Island, in relation to New York, 9
New York, in relation to Chicago, 14
toward the park from Myrtle's
apartment, 40
seaboard, in relation to frontier
brothel and saloon, 106
train movement away from
Louisville, 160
East, the [location]; See West, the
Nick returns from, 6
Nick goes to, 7, 24
Nick will stay in, 14
Gatsby liked it, 176
haunted, 185

East Egg
the white palaces of fashionable, 10
Nick drives to, 10-11
condescending to West Egg, 49
East Eggers, 31
Eberhardt, Mrs., 35
Eckleburg, Doctor. T. J., 27-28, 30, 129, 167
ectoplasm, 34; See ghost
Edgar, 174
egg, eggs. See West Egg; East Egg;
white; photograph of hen; gonnegtion
hard-boiled painting, 7
a pair of enormous, 9
in the Columbus story, 9
egotism, 25
electric stove, 8
electrocuted, killers of Rosenthal, 75
elevator boy, 33, 42, 178
El Greco, 185
England, 79, 97, 136
Englishmen, young, at Gatsby's, 46
English oak, 49
equal; See unequal
euphemisms, the old, chafed under, 114
Europe, 38, 70, 73
Ewing; See Klipspringer
exploration
Nick as guide, pathfinder, original
settler, 8
Columbus, 9
Dutch sailors, 189
eye, eyes
of Tom, 11, 111, 125
of Jordan, 15, 63
of Daisy on her finger, 16
impersonal, 17
Daisy winks, 18
avoiding all, 20
Daisy's look into the dusk, 21
Daisy's flash, 22
of Doctor. T. J. Eckleburg, 27-28,
129, 131, 167
Myrtle looks Tom flush in the, 30
Myrtle's regal glance, 32-33

# Losing the Virginity of Time: The Literary Coordinates of Bruno Schulz and Isaac Babel

Ryan Boudinot

The absurd fever dream of modernity that Kafka wrought in prose was endured in the lives of Bruno Schulz and Isaac Babel. Both twentieth century Jewish writers, Babel and Schulz suffered religious and political persecution, met violent deaths, and changed world literature. One was a metaphysician, the other a hardboiled realist. One enjoyed the accolades of the greatest artists of his time, the other toiled mostly in obscurity. One saw the world, the other was afraid to leave his hometown. Both left us with painfully incomplete bodies of work.

Born into the merchant class in the Polish city of Drohobycz, Bruno Schulz became a school teacher of art, drafting, and writing. Although he lived to see his work published, he never achieved a level of success that would have allowed him to retire from academia. In his journal he bemoaned the demands on his time made by his day job, which he needed to support his family. He cherished what he called "the virginity of time," a state of blessed second childhood in which his sole intellectual responsibility was the cultivation of his imagination. A fast reader could consume what remains of the life work of Bruno Schulz in a long, sunlit day. A translator of Kafka's *The Trial*, Schulz wrote and illustrated two collections of short stories, *The Street of Crocodiles* (also known as *Cinnamon Shops*) and *Sanatorium Under the Sign of the Hourglass*, and many letters to the few distant admirers who recognized his gifts during his lifetime.

Between 1939 and 1942, Drohobycz was occupied first by Germans, then Russians, then Germans again. Schulz at first was able to continue work as a teacher, but during the second German occupation was denied regular employment. He formally requested status as a "necessary Jew," submitting his artwork to the Judenrat. A Gestapo officer named Felix Landau, impressed by Schulz's drawings, personally sponsored the artist, granting him a classification of skilled worker. In addition to the murals and portraits Schulz created for Landau, he was assigned to work in a retirement home categorizing confiscated books, his efforts in part helping the Nazis determine what books were to be destroyed.

When Schulz and his family were moved into the Drohobycz ghetto, he gave his manuscripts and drawings to those who were in a better position to protect them, so-called "Catholics outside the ghetto" who remain unknown. Friends in literary circles in Warsaw were unable to convince him to escape, as he was alternately wracked with the fear of being caught while fleeing and hopeful that his relationship with Landau would protect him. Ten days before he died, Schulz met an acquaintance named

Michal Mirski in the street. According to Mirski, Schulz carried a manuscript of notes about one hundred pages long, which he described as a work about the most awful martyrdom in history.

Around 11:00 A.M. on November 19, 1942, the date some Warsaw friends were to finally help him escape Drohobycz, Bruno Schulz found himself in the ghetto during a Gestapo shooting spree. An officer named Karl Gunther, angry that Landau had killed one of "his Jews," a dentist named Low, used the opportunity to settle the score by shooting Schulz twice in the head.

Schulz's prose is a relentless drilling down through individual memory toward the mythic, an act of channeling where "man is only a transit station, a temporary junction of mesmeric currents, wandering hither and thither within the lap of eternal matter"[1] With his stories and drawings as his vehicle, Schulz sought a method to "mature into childhood" and enter a state of ego obliteration in which he could access the mythic interface of all that remains unknowable. There are few static, empirically solid physical objects in Schulz's work; everything trembles on the edge of transformation. Nothing in Schulz's universe is more transformative and dynamic than literature itself. *Sanatorium Under the Sign of the Hourglass* begins with a description of an incredible volume, the Platonic source of all other books, a monomythic everybook whose pages literally move with life:

> Sometimes my father would wander off and leave me alone with The Book;
> the wind would rustle through its pages and the pictures would rise. And as
> the windswept pages were turned, merging the colors and shapes, a shiver
> ran through the columns of text, freeing from among the letters flocks of
> swallows and larks.[2]

In the Schulzian plane, street children turn into sages, musical instruments play themselves, the historical figures preserved in stamp albums move within their borders. When Joseph in *Sanatorium* reads about wild animals, Schulz is not satisfied to depict him merely sitting in a room with a static text in his lap. Rather there's a smearing of setting in which what the character reads spills off the page, takes three-dimensional shape, fills the room with a procession of beasts. Here Schulz stakes his aesthetic territory between the empirical limits of typography and what happens in the mind, particularly visually, during the reading experience. It feels appropriate that the original illustrations that Schulz included with his stories feature figures with preternaturally large heads on stunted bodies, as though to suggest the writer could barely contain all he envi-

---

[1] The Street of Crocodiles, *"The Comet," Penguin, 1977, p 147*

[2] Sanatorium Under the Sign of the Hourglass, *Penguin, 1977, p 1*

sioned in his own.

Despite the richness of the work of Schulz in print, many readers remain haunted by the loss of what promised to be his life's masterpiece, presumably those 100 embryonic pages he carried with him in the last days of his life, the lost novel titled *The Messiah*. No one is certain how complete the manuscript was when Schulz was murdered, or whether it still exists (there are rumors that it is in storage/lost in the KGB archives). The novel allegedly opens in a small town populated by characters who have been informed that the messiah is soon to arrive.

The search for *The Messiah* has been the life work of Jerzy Ficowski, a Polish scholar who was enraptured by Schulz's stories as a teenager, and who continues to search for Schulz's lost fiction and visual art. Ficowski's biography and deeply personal consideration of Schulz's work, *Regions of the Great Heresy*, published last year in translation, joined a corpus of work that surrounds Schulz's labyrinthine stories like a protective membrane. At least two novelists have taken it upon themselves to imagine Schulz in a fictional setting; David Grossman's *See Under: Love* concerns the adult son of Holocaust survivors who believes he is channeling the work of the late Schulz. In *The Messiah of Stockholm*, Cynthia Ozick goes a step further, presenting us with a Swiss journalist who is the fictional offspring of the artist himself. A battered manuscript of *The Messiah* actually appears in Ozick's novel, and she indulges herself (and us) by attempting to imagine the experience of reading it. Then, as if to punish herself for such a blasphemous act, she makes sure the manuscript is destroyed. From this daydream we're left where we started, with a hole in the world of books where a masterpiece should be.

Cynthia Ozick also provides the introduction to *The Complete Works of Isaac Babel*, a volume tenderly assembled by the Russian author's daughter Nathalie, published in 2002. Ozick rightly places Babel in the company of Kafka, pointing out that their dissimilarities provide us with coordinates that tell us "what we in our time are obliged to know about the brutal tracings of force and deception, including self-deception."[3] Bruno Schulz may also serve as a useful coordinate in relation to Babel. Where Schulz was insular, quiet, enamored with the innocence of childhood, Babel was bold, spirited, obnoxious even. Where Schulz's drawings seem to indicate a self-conscious man masochistically in thrall of female sexual power, Babel fathered three children (that we know of) by three different women, one of whom he was married to. Where Schulz enjoyed modest fame, Babel's fame was a burst that was subsequently erased from history. He's been coming back.

Isaac Babel grew up in the port city of Odessa, where he endured the Czarist legal limitations, including limits on his education, that accompa-

---

[3] The Complete Works of Isaac Babel, *Introduction by Cynthia Ozick, Norton, 2002, p 14*

nied his happening to be Jewish. Odessa is the setting of his "Benya Krik" stories in which a cast of insouciant gangsters behave in a sort of cocksure, proto-Quentin Tarantino manner, if you can imagine a Tarantino character of Russian Jewish heritage, circa 1923. A typical line of dialogue:

"'Life is shit,' he muttered, 'The world's a brothel, everyone's a swindler!'"[4]

In *The Odessa Stories* lies the kernel of Babel's fascination with brutality, yet he has not yet begun to appreciate the spiritual toll of bloodshed. In the 20s, Babel's great theme would deepen, owing to his role as a war correspondent and propagandist traveling with the Red Calvalry into Poland. That year, while Bruno Schulz concentrated on pulling his drawings together into a portfolio to reproduce and give to friends, Babel worked for a newspaper called *The Red Cavalryman*, rousing troops with such exhortations as:

> The dogs that haven't yet been completely slashed to pieces have begun howling coarsely. The murderers who haven't yet been completely clubbed to death are crawling out of their graves . . . Slaughter them, Red Army fighters! Stamp harder on the rising lids of their rancid coffins![5]

Propagandist.[6] The designation gives one pause when considering Babel's oeuvre. There are at least three ways to consider how Babel's knack for inspiring his countrymen's bloodlust figures into his overall body of work. One knee-jerk reaction would be to disregard the rest of his stories as stemming from a hack who'd reprehensibly sold out. A more charitable view would be to permit that he simply applied his naturally bestowed gifts to survive in a society in the throes of chaotic and unprecedented transformation, and that it would be arrogant of us to pass judgment on these supposed transgressions from our twenty-first-century American perch. But the works that Babel published after his stint as war correspondent suggest a third interpretation of the experience. Acutely aware of the terrible power of rhetoric, Babel turned his blades against the exaggerations he had perpetuated and demanded, through his fiction, the truth. The result is Babel's masterpiece, the *Red Cavalry* story cycle. The procession of vignettes rattles between the covers like bursts of machine gun fire. Vivid horror follows vivid horror. In one scene, a soldier relieving himself outside at night discovers that he's been pissing into the face of a corpse. The brutality the cavalrymen inflict on a goose or hives of bees is rendered as gravely and brutally as that which is inflicted on human targets. In "Salt," arguably the best story of the collection, a

---

[4] The Complete Works of Isaac Babel, *Norton, 2002, p 179*

[5] ibid, *p 373*

[6] To be fair, I should note that Bruno Schulz, for his part, was also a propagandist responsible for painting patriotic murals during the Russian occupation, although he elicited sharp rebukes from his bosses when he "over-used" the colors of the Ukrainian flag in a particular composition.

group of soldiers on a train bestows its generosity and then its wrath on a woman whose bundle turns out to be smuggled salt instead of a baby, as they've been led to believe. The vengeance they deliver for being deceived is as cold-blooded as any act of literary violence one is likely to ever read.

Babel delivers the vulgarity of wartime with a keen eye for the poetic details that have nothing to do with violence; a contemporary comparison could be Terrence Mallick's film *The Thin Red Line*, in which the camera takes in the delicate foliage of the battlefield as intently as the horrors visited upon it. Reading Babel on war is a *beautiful* experience, and he knows it, and he exploits the horrible confusion and tension we feel as he grabs us by the neck and forces us to look. The crimes he documents are not so much crimes against warring political tribes as against the entire natural order upon which civilization prospers. Agonizingly, he concludes the story "After the Battle" with a description of a ravaged community and the untenable demand that war has placed on the narrator's morality:

> The village floated and bulged, crimson clay oozing from its gloomy wounds. The first star flashed above me and tumbled in the clouds. The rain whipped the willow trees and dwindled. This evening soared into the sky like a flock of birds and darkness laid its wet garland upon me. I was exhausted, and, crouching beneath the crown of death, walked on, begging fate for the simplest ability—the ability to kill a man.

In *Red Cavalry*, Babel named names, peopling the tales with real figures like General Budyonny, who, naturally, objected fiercely to his portrayal as foolish and inarticulate. Babel accused another real figure, the military commissar Voroshilov, of poor military strategy. Unfortunately for Babel, Budyonny would later become the Soviet Union's first deputy commisar for defense, and Voroshilov—a personal friend of Stalin's—would become head of state. Uh-oh.

And so a journalist who wrote exaggerations became an artist who leveled his condemnation of wartime atrocities through fiction. Perhaps *condemnation* is the wrong word. Babel seems ambivalent in places, simultaneously attracted and repelled by the horror that was his theme. At times one suspects he is getting off on it. And lots of other Russians got off on it, too. In his lifetime, Babel claimed the mantle of Russia's greatest writer. Befriended by the literary lions of the era, including Maxim Gorky, Andre Gide, and Andre Malraux, in 1935 Babel was invited to represent his country at the International Congress of Writers for the Defense of Culture and Peace in Paris. Conversely, three years later, when Bruno Schulz saved enough money to travel to Paris during his summer break, he found the city practically deserted. Nearly everyone the Polish writer had wanted to meet was in the country on vacation.

Isaac Babel was fortunate enough to find himself in a position in which he could argue against fascism and tyranny, and he didn't hesitate to seize the opportunity. Critical of Stalin both within Russia and internationally, he refused to bow to the official version of history being written by those who achieved their power through might and steel. Babel was arrested on espionage charges on May 15, 1939, based on evidence supplied by other writers who had been arrested and interrogated before him. Eight months later he was woken in his cell at 1:40 A.M. at Moscow's Lubyanka prison and executed before a firing squad.

Eight years after Babel's death, rumors were still circulating about his release from prison. When he was officially exonerated and details of his death were made public in the '50s, Babel's last recorded words emerged, chillingly, from long-hidden official documents, *"Let me finish my work."*

It's a plea that's easy to imagine coming from the mouth of Bruno Schulz in his final moments in the streets of Drohobycz. Babel and Schulz never knew each other, but their lives form two sides of a double helix, a system of artistic divergences, intensity of vision, and suffering. The burden of these artists' deaths lies squarely on the shoulders of empire. While we may still hold out hope that *The Messiah* will yet arrive, the responsibility now rests squarely with readers as stewards of their legacies. Their work is ours to finish. ✧

# Elizabeth Searle
Sherry Ellis

Elizabeth Searle is the author of *Celebrities in Disgrace*, a finalist for the
Paterson Fiction Prize; *A Four Sided Bed*, nominated for an American
Library Association Award; and a short story collection, *My Body to You*,
which won the Iowa Short Fiction Award. Her short stories have
appeared in *Ploughshares, Michigan Quarterly, Agni, Kenyon Review*, and
*Redbook*. She teaches writing at the Stonecoast M.F.A. program and at
Emerson College.

**SHERRY ELLIS:** In *Celebrities in Disgrace*, many of the female characters
are preoccupied with fame and a hunger for attention—being seen and
being watched. What are the challenges of writing about this theme?

**ELIZABETH SEARLE:** Ambition and women is something I had not
written about in any realistic, sympathetic, in-depth way before, and it's
easy to satirize. One reason for the theme of *Celebrities in Disgrace* is
what I have observed to be the obsessive need for attention. I taught
special education for a while and noticed that this is the common denom-
inator of all people. The phrase is used, "they're trying to get attention,"
and it seems that so often the motives of people center on the need for
attention. I'm writing a novel now, in which the siblings struggle for
notice. I think the challenges are that it is one of those things that people
don't want to talk about, and also portraying the characters so they are
somewhat sympathetic.

I have a phrase in my mind, "the witch of ambition," and I do think
there is this sort of dark force inside of people and any of those dark
forces are hard to write about but they're the ones you want to write
about. It seems like such a driving force of our time. *Celebrities in
Disgrace* is a book where I started with the title, it came to me during the
time of Nancy and Tanya. It is hard to make the characters sympathetic
when they are that ambitious, and it is hard to get past that and not make
them shallow caricatures.

Q: "Celebrities in Disgrace" is both the title of your book and your novella.
In the novella, a struggling actress, who is elated to believe that her career
is about to take off, becomes vulnerable and "the accused." How did you
juxtapose the events in this novella for maximum impact?

A: Oh, that novella was so much fun to write; it was the most fun writing
experience I've ever had. During the era of Nancy and Tanya, I was
obsessed by it. It was this "girl thing," the pretty skirts, and I remember
there was a quote in the Boston *Globe* that got me thinking about it that I
use in the novella: "America's full of Tonyas who want to be Nancys."

During the scandal my friends would clip articles and send them to me. I didn't know what I was going to do with them; I just knew I wanted a lot of information. That's what always happens; you have one thing you're thinking about and then another totally different thing happens and you band them together and something happens. I had the title in my mind even before the "Nancy/Tonya thing," and it all connected with Lowell, Massachusetts. I had some connection with people doing repertory theater there, and I had done some theater in high school and at Arizona State where I went to college, and I wanted to write about it. Then I heard that while the "Nancy/Tonya thing" was still happening, producers were already casting a movie, even before it resolved itself. That stuck in my mind and that triggered the novella. I thought "what if" I wanted to write about a struggling actress and wondered how could I make it happen during the week of the scandal.

Q: The novella "Celebrities in Disgrace" begins, "He stapled his face over hers. In the subzero dawn of Skate-Off Day—7 A.M. in Lowell, 1 P.M. in Lillehammer—the staples shot back at him, the kiosk's corkboard as ungiving as ice." Through this image the reader can almost feel the cold, can almost feel the staples. Do you frequently use metaphor to evoke a physical response on the part of the reader?

A: Sense memories are important, I think; you can convince the reader of almost anything if you connect it to their sense memories and I always think in terms of how the reader is feeling. I always try to get physical immediately, to evoke physical sensations, to be very concrete and very sensual. I feel things when I'm reading, so that's very important to me.

I used to read for the blind and I used hearing the typing machines in a story, printing the Braille, it's a terrifying sound; the whole story is in that repeated rhythm. I always try to put sounds in my stories.

Q: In the poem "The Road Not Taken" Robert Frost wrote, "Two roads diverged in a yellow wood/And sorry I could not travel both..." Your short story "101" is about a young woman who contemplates dramatic changes in her life as she approaches an intersection. "I approached an intersection, poised my foot over my brake, thinking the way my dad had taught me, *Stop, Stop, Stop*, then as the light stayed yellow and I floored the gas, *Go no matter what.*" Do you frequently use metaphor to evoke an emotional response?

A: Oh, yes, definitely. I think it's very hard to write about emotions in the abstract. I'm always telling my students to find some physical thing that their characters can be doing. I can remember having a breakthrough with my editor at Graywolf, when she was trying to get me to show emotions.

I had just been abstractly describing it, and we figured out that a character was mad at her husband—he was gone, and she decided she was going to sleep on the couch; she tried to unfold the bed and then she couldn't, she started hitting it, and then she tried to fold it back up but she couldn't. That was so much better than what I had written before.

I use the theme of the road diverging often. In my novel I have girl "A" and girl "B." I love doubles in fiction, two characters that are similar but follow their diverging paths. And in this story, "101," the use of the intersection seemed to be a good way to say the character is plunging forward no matter what.

Q: In *The Joy of Writing Sex*, Elizabeth Benedict states, "A well-written sex scene engages us on many levels: erotic, aesthetic, psychological, metaphorical, even philosophical." Do you agree with these criteria?

A: I agree with it completely. I used Benedict's book for my master's level seminar at Stonecoast, called *The Erotic Pen*. So-called erotic writing does not work for me if it is not connected to real characters and does not contain emotional content.

I'm in the early stages of trying to put together an anthology, and one possible slant we might take is to call it "Not Erotica." The word "erotica" seems to be used to describe work that is written just to put a sex scene together, that isn't connected to the larger work.

Q: "101" ends with the primary character holding an ostrich egg shard as she drives back to Phoenix. The next story in the collection, *Celebrities In Disgrace*, "Celebration," begins with the sentence, "Cracking an egg for her husband's birthday cake, Sarah spread her thumb and index finger so the white stretched." In "Round Objects" from your collection *My Body to You*, you write, "She lies still as an egg. A heavy egg hidden in a hole." As a writer how do you find symbols for your characters or do the symbols become apparent to you from the stories themselves?

A: I love eggs and I'm fascinated by visceral and primal things, and I'm always putting them in my stories. It seems that you don't choose the symbols; they just keep coming up over and over again. I believe that the things that stick out in your mind and you're not sure why, are the perfect fiction material. There are often babies, missing babies, and things having to do with the female body in my work; my story "White Eggplant" is another example.

I give an exercise to my students to help them free-associate about objects or animals in their stories that they think are important or charged. I always use as an example something that was really helpful to me in writing the short story, "My Body to You"—free-associating about the whippet. I knew I needed a dog in this story, but at first I didn't know why I made it a whippet. I thought, okay, the whippet has a greyhound shape, it's like a woman's body, but it's all hard, it's not at all soft. And just thinking that—suddenly the whippet made sense to me, and I thought—this is why I have the description on the subway where everyone's flesh is jiggling—the character hates that and she's sort of starving herself. I also free-associated about a friend, whose sister was "going berserk," who called and came over to our house, and when she got in her car the only thing she grabbed was her dog. That became a big scene in "My Body to You," when the character escapes from her house and takes only the dog with her. The other thing I got out of thinking about the whippet was my last line, where the character is looking at the bodies of the airplanes, that are so sleek, and she thinks that they are like whippets waiting to run—and she is about to take off too; it makes her feel for a minute that flying is a perfectly natural act.

Q: You said about *A Four Sided Bed*: "My novel was also inspired by the singer k.d. lang, who says that she sets out to 'seduce' her whole audience." When you wrote this novel how did you attempt to achieve this goal?

A: Oh, I had that very specifically in mind. I was fascinated by k.d. lang during the writing of this book and she was such an inspiration. In *A Four Sided Bed* there are three-person love scenes, there's a homo-erotic element, there's a hetero-erotic element, there's sort of something for everything. I thought there was a chance to write sex scenes that could turn on practically anyone, hook them in. And so you set yourself a challenge that is really interesting to you. I saw k.d. lang as a lesbian performer who was very welcoming, not only singing to "her" group. In other ways I felt very nervous, treading on this territory, but I loved having a challenge in writing the sex scenes. Yes, that was a real overt goal of mine.

Q: Are there things that you would be afraid of writing about?

A: My husband sometimes quotes a line from the movie *Tootsie* where Dustin Hoffman is thinking of something awful or shocking he can do on camera to get out of his soap opera and someone says to him, "I can't think of anything sick and disgusting you haven't done already."

I haven't tackled the theme of violence too extensively, although there is a scene of violence in my new book, and I don't do strictly autobiographical material, as I would be afraid of hurting people too much. I do take a lot of autobiographical material and use it as a springboard.

**Q:** How does your process vary in writing a story or a novel?

**A:** It's a whole different thing. For me a novel involves thinking about a story for a couple of years before actually writing it. I take characters and try them out. And then there is a whole first draft, and rewriting, which I have to do a lot of, because I tend to write dense and long. I cut things down an incredible amount, so it is just such a huge undertaking, whereas with short stories everything is reduced. I might think of it for months in advance, and work on it for months, although if you added it all together it might be years that I've worked on the same story. I take something like a big six-month run at it, and then time passes and I look at it again. Short stories are more manageable. They're fun in that you can know a few important things about your character and have a story, whereas in a novel you have to do so much more character work. A novel is a long, long trance; it takes over your whole life. You have to push though and keep the threads going. Short stories are so instinctive; it's more like putting a poem together; in some ways, I don't like them ending so soon. A novella is a fun mix of the two. You can get immersed but it's not so unyielding.

**Q:** You use the title "The Young and the Rest of Us" both for a short story in *Celebrities in Disgrace* and as the title for a chapter in *A Four Sided Bed*. How difficult is it to return to familiar territory and yet change the meaning of the material?

**A:** *The Young and the Restless* was so much a part of my childhood. I could not do anything without that show. I hate typing, and for the past twenty years I have taped it and then listened to it while I transcribe my long-hand to typed form. Maybe I'm fooling myself, but as an otherwise "literary writer," I believe that I have learned a lot from that show about plot. I picture it like a stove, something simmering here, different plots, and I imagine which one was on the front burner, the back burner, on boil, which is a helpful technique when you're writing a novel and you are trying to develop different plots and have them converge. In each scene, *The Young and the Restless* puts in a hook, and the rhythms of the plot get into your brain.

**Q:** For the past three years you have served as mistress of ceremonies at a Valentine's Day eve festivity in Boston, where writers read their work, "The Erotic Pen: Passion, Eros and Naked Lust," hosted by PEN/New England. How did you conceive of this literary celebration and how has it been received?

**A:** I came up with the idea of this event as a board member of PEN/New England; serving on this board is such an honor and a privilege. I wondered what would be the dream event that I would want to see, and I love high-quality writing about sex. We got Jayne Anne Phillips and Maria Flook, our first year, who are literally two of my favorite writers—and I read that first time too, a loss of virginity piece, and Andre Dubus III for the second year. It is a literary event but it also has this fun, sexy element that people love and people who don't ordinarily go to readings can enjoy.

Q: Carl Jung said "the meeting of two personalities is like the contact of two chemical substances, if there is any reaction, both are transformed." How does the interaction between characters in your stories and novel result in transformation?

A: I always think in terms of ramming two characters together and seeing what happens. I think what helped me with my novel *A Four Sided Bed*, and what my editor at Graywolf showed me, is that there had to be a spark of transformation for Alice, the wife character, what happens to her; I already had an understanding of what happened when J.J., Kin and Bird came together. I always seem to have two female characters; I have two sisters in the novel I'm working on now, and girl "A" and girl "B" in *A Four Sided Bed*. I like to have characters come up to each other and come to know each other in different ways.

Q: What advice do you have for new writers?

A: The standard: read, read and read! If you don't find yourself to be some-one who loves to read, and to be excited by what you read, you might be barking up the wrong tree for a form of expression. You have to enjoy the process itself. Of course we know that the publishing life is very difficult; writing has to be satisfying in itself. I would advise new writers to seek out workshops. You have to have other people looking at your work to move forward. When I was a theater major I remember a teacher saying, if there is something else you guys can do, do it. This is only for you if you can't live without it, and I thought about acting, and wondered, whereas I did feel this way about writing—that I couldn't not do it. Writing can be very satisfying, if you are a serious reader, to explore it, give it a serious shot. It is somewhat like a religion; it can give you tremendous spiritual satisfaction.

Q: Which writers have most influenced your work?

A: Virginia Woolf, I was really struck by her in college; *Them* by Joyce Carol Oates when I was a teenager, I cannot imagine not having read her; Alice Munro; James Salter, who by coincidence wound up being the judge of the Iowa competition; Don Delillo; David Foster Wallace, who I think is very hilarious; Rick Moody; so many contemporary writers: Mary

Gaitskill; Maria Flook; there are really sensual female writers, they are my favorite kind of writers.

Q: What are some of the common problems you find in your students' work?

A: I agree with something David Huddle said in his book *The Writing Habit*: in fact, I'm doing my seminar at Stonecoast this semester based on seventy-seven autobiographical questions he gives his students, that are designed to elicit concrete memories. He says that sometimes students work is so unconnected to their real lives that they are not invested in it—there's a kind of slinging things around and shooting people left and right. Huddle says that they are writing from their false selves. You have to find a natural voice for yourself. Huddle suggests that when you help students start with the real material from their lives, that they care about it more. Often when people start writing they get stilted, or self-conscious. It is hard to find a way to tell a story in a voice that is natural to you.

Q: In a recent *Poets and Writers* article in which Jeffrey Skinner discussed revision, he said, "writing is revision and yet each time I suggest revisions to a student or a friend, each time I face what remains to be done in my own writing, I feel the specter of resistance rising anew." Do you resist the process of revision?

A: I don't resist it anymore. I did when I was younger, which I regret; I could have done so much better. I agree with something Janet Burroway said, that revision is "more dreaded than dreadful." Now I see that I know how to get my prose under control, it tends to be very dense at first, the drafts I would not show to anyone but my husband, you have to hack through them with a knife practically; I actually like doing revision. I boiled the 500 pages that I had for *A Four Sided Bed* down to 300, not cutting a single whole scene, just taking words out. It takes a long time to get a sense of how to edit yourself. Students who really balk at it and refuse to do revision won't reach a publishable level; the ones that are willing to give in, go over and over it again, that's what it takes.

Q: E.M. Forster said, "Some reviews give pain. That is regrettable, but no author has the right to whine. He invited publicity and he must take the publicity that comes along." When you read reviews of your work, how do you cope with negativity?

A: I agree about not having the right to whine. Especially in this age, you are so lucky to be published. I think it is a privilege to have these problems. But at the same time I think that every review I've read takes a year off my life. To have that helpless feeling of knowing that this is the way it is going to be presented to the world. But even the bad reviews I've gotten have had good things in them. It's a very emotional experience to have people react to your work in print. Of course it can hurt, but sometimes you look back at it later and see that there's some truth in it.

Q: What are you working on now?

A: A novel about an aspiring actress who half-accidentally lost her virginity on camera, which comes back to haunt her in different ways. The political family that she has come from has given her competitive drive. Something violent is triggered by an autistic character who is obsessed with John Hinkley, Jr., almost an assassination attempt. I've just got to figure it out. ✧

## Twenty Questions
## TOM PERROTTA

POST ROAD invites its readers to submit questions for Tom Perrotta, author of the novels *Little Children, Joe College, Election* (which was made into an acclaimed movie starring Matthew Broderick and Reese Witherspoon), *The Wishbones,* and the short story collection *Bad Haircut.* Mr. Perrotta has taught writing at Yale and Harvard, and has worked as a screenwriter and journalist. His nonfiction work has appeared recently in *Rolling Stone* and *GQ.* He grew up in New Jersey and now lives outside Boston.

Please submit your questions to twentyquestions@postroadmag.com before August 1. POST ROAD will select twenty questions and publish them, along with Mr. Perrotta's answers, in an upcoming issue. Those whose questions are selected will receive a complimentary copy of the issue in which the interview appears.

# where boston gets writing.

boston's best writing workshops
master classes
author-hosted book club
"after the mfa" event series
"saturday morning cereal" discussions
readings & open mikes
fellowships
& more...

## grub street, inc.
boston's independent writing center
561 windsor street
somerville, ma 02143

### 617.623.8100
### www.grubstreet.org